Anonymous

Rules and Constitutions for the Ursuline Religious

Of the Presentation of Our Blessed Lady

Anonymous

Rules and Constitutions for the Ursuline Religious
Of the Presentation of Our Blessed Lady

ISBN/EAN: 9783337119355

Printed in Europe, USA, Canada, Australia, Japan

Cover: Foto ©Lupo / pixelio.de

More available books at **www.hansebooks.com**

RULES

AND

CONSTITUTIONS

FOR THE

URSULINE RELIGIOUS

OF THE

PRESENTATION OF OUR BLESSED LADY.

WITH INSTRUCTIONS ON THE SAME.

Translated from the French Edition of 1827, by the Ursulines of Galveston.

NEW ORLEANS:
T. FITZWILLIAM & CO., PRINTERS, 62 CAMP STREET,
1885.

☦

A. M. D. G.

Approbation of the Translation.

The Rules and Constitutions of the Ursuline Religious of the Presentation of our Blessed Lady,—translated by the Ursulines of Galveston—having been carefully examined by the Rev. Jesuit Fathers of this City, and declared by them, a faithful version of the original French Edition.

We hereby approve their being printed and circulated in the Houses of the Order.

Given at St. Ursula's Monastery, Galveston, July 23, 1885.

† N. A. GALLAGHER,
Bp. Adm. of Galveston.

Approbations of the Original Constitutions.

I.

"We, Nicholas, by the Mercy of God and the favor
" of the Apostolic See, Bishop and Count of Usez,—
" having read and examined the present Constitutions
" of the Ursuline Religious of the Presentation of
" our Lady, under the Rule of St. Augustin; and hav-
" ing found therein nothing contrary to the holy
" canons and apostolic constitutions, but rather prac-
" tices of piety most suitable to the duties and the
" state to which these nuns have been called, and well
" calculated to form souls to Religious Perfection, we
" do hereby approve, confirm and authorize the same.
" Given at Usez, May 27, 1641."

"†NICHOLAS, Bp. of Usez."

II.

" Nos, Franciscus de Gabrielis, juris utriusque Doc-
" tor, Protonotarius Apostolicus, Canonicus Ecclesiæ
" Cathedralis Cavalliensis, Datarius Legationis Aveni-
" onensis, Vicarius et Officialis generalis Illustrissimi
" et Reverendissimi Domini Marii Philornardi, Archie-
" piscopi Avenionensis, visis præsentibus *Constitutioni-*
" *bus Monialium Sanctæ Ursulæ, militantium sub Regula*
" *Sancti Augustini erectarum sub invocatione Præsenta-*
" *tionis sacratissimæ Virginis Mariæ.* Cum dictæ Consti-
" tutiones sint valde piæ et religiosæ, et nullo modo
" adversentur sacris Canonibus et dispositioni Concilii
" Tridentini, et Constitutionum Apostolicarum, illas
" de voto Reverendi Patris Rectoris Societatis Jesu, et
" Reverendi Domini Ludovici à Vento in sacra Theolo-
" gia Doctoris, approbamus confirmamus, et autorisa-
" mus."

" Datum Avenione, die 22 Februarii, 1641."
" FRANCISCUS DE GABRIELIS,"
" Vicarius Generalis Avenionensis."
" JOANNES BAPTISTA GUESNAY,"
" Rector et Theologus Societatis Jesu."
" LUDOVICUS A VENTO,"
" Doctor et Theologus."

" We, Benedict Puys, Doctor of Theology, Sacristan
" and Canon of the Collegiate Church of St. Nizier,
" Lyons, and Lieutenant of the Primacy of France,
" have read the *Instructions* on the Rules and Consti-
" tutions of the Ursuline Religious of the Presentation

" of our Lady, and have found therein nothing but
" what is conformable to christian faith and piety.
"Given at Lyons, this 11th day of July, 1643.
"BENEDICT PUYS."

IV.

" I, the undersigned Doctor of Divinity, certify to
" having read a Book entitled " *Instructions for the*
" *Ursuline Religious of the Presentation of our Lady*,
" wherein, far from noticing anything contrary to
" the belief of the Roman Catholic Church,—I have
" found a most solid doctrine, well calculated to lead
" Religious persons to perfection.
"Lyons, this 11th day of July, 1643.
"FRANCIS ROMANI."

Approbation of the Revised Edition, 1827.

" Joseph Rosati, of the Congregation of the Mis-
" sions, by the grace of God and the authority of the
" holy Apostolic See, Bishop of Tanagra and Admin-
" istrator of New Orleans and St. Louis.

" Having observed, during the Pastoral Visitation
" made in the Convent of the Presentation belonging
" to the Ursulines of New Orleans, that sundry Arti-
" cles of their Constitutions could not be observed in
" their Community, owing to very grave difficulties
" arising from the situation of their Monastery, and
" from the climate and customs of the country; per-
" ceiving, moreover, that for these reasons, our prede-
" cessors, the Bishops and Ecclesiastical Superiors,

" had authorized the Religious to yield to the neces-
" sity which prevented them from observing the afore-
" mentioned articles of their Constitutions, we have
" deemed it necessary for the greater tranuqillity of
" the Sisters' conscience, that they modify these seve-
" ral points in such a manner as to make them practi-
" cable. This having been faithfully executed in
" accordance with our intentions, we hereby confirm
" and approve all that has been changed in the Con-
" stitutions—and this all the more willingly, as these
" changes do not affect the spirit, or any of the essen-
" tial points of the Institute. We permit the Supe-
" rioress to have a new Edition of the Rules and Con-
" stitutions issued, conformable to the model that has
" been revised and corrected. We desire, moreover,
" that the new edition be distributed among the Sis-
" ters as soon as received, and that it be recognized
" and observed as the only Rule in vigor within the
" Monastery.

" Given at New Orleans, this 31st day of May, 1827.

† JOSEPH,

" Bishop of St. Louis and Adm. of New Orleans."

PREFACE.

Our holy Mother, the Church, is compared to an army drawn up in battle array, and divided into several companies. As each Religious congregation should follow the standard of one of the Founders of Religious Orders, that of the Ursulines is to march under the Rule of the glorious Father and Doctor of the Church, St. Augustin, one of the four Patriarchs and first Founders of Religious Orders.

Following the example of St. Angela who laid the first foundation of this Company in the city of Brescia, in Italy, they have selected St. Ursula as their Patroness, in order that, as it pleased God to give, through her example and exhortation, the crown of martyrdom and virginity to her companions, so may this devout Institute through her intercession, draw many souls to the service of Him who is the Crown of Virgins. This Congregation of Ursulines has, however, a distinctive mark; for, in virtue of the Bull of our Holy Father, Urban VIII, given at Rome, Feb. 5th, 1637, and by the authority of the venerable Prelates in whose dioceses it has been established, said congregation offers and dedicates itself to our Blessed Lady presented in the Temple,—who, as the Queen of Virgins, was the first to offer to God, on the occasion of her presentation, the agreeable holocaust of her

Virginal purity,—and who drew after her, by the sweet odor of her virtues, so many thousands of pure virgins. Hence, this Congregation has received the title of *Ursulines of the Presentation of Our Lady*—a title most appropriate to this Institute; for, as the Blessed Virgin was drawn into the Temple by a special attraction from God, to be there prepared by the Holy Ghost, to become His most worthy Mother, so is this Congregation wholly consecrated to God, in order that young girls may be prepared in it, by the holy instructions they receive from their tenderest years, to become worthy Temples of God, who wishes to dwell in them by His grace, and Tabernacles of Jesus Christ whom they should receive frequently in the adorable sacrament of the Altar. Moreover, those who have been called to the Religious life, professed in this Institute, are themselves prepared to become, as it were, the Mothers of God; for, by the instructions they impart, they form and cause Jesus to take birth in the souls confided to their charge. Hereby are manifested the dignity and efficacy of this Institute, as also the obligation incumbent on those who have been called to it, to work with fidelity in functions so holy and sublime.

This Congregation has subsisted during the past forty-seven years, that is, since about 1595, in the practice of every Christian virtue—making only the vow of chastity, with the simple promise of Poverty and Obedience. Now, as it has pleased God to inspire the Religious with a desire to join to their holy exercises, the three vows of Religion, these Constitutions have been drawn up, conformably to what they have hitherto practised, adding only what regards the obligations of the Religious life which they have embraced.

These Constitutions are, therefore, to be regarded not as coming from the hand of man or directed by human prudence, but as dictated and ordained by the spirit of Jesus who always abides with His Church, to direct and govern it, and who takes a special care of the Virgins consecrated to Him, and who are, according to St. Cyprian, the choicest portion of His flock. These Constitutions should be regarded by the members of this Institute, as was the pillar of fire among the Israelites,—for they are destined to lead those who observe them, through the darkness and wilderness of this life, to their true land of promise—the possession of God. The path may seem difficult, but Jesus, our Lord, walks before us, inviting us both by word and example to carry our cross and to follow Him and His blessed Mother, who treading in His sacred footsteps, has drawn so many virgins in her train.

St. Ursula and her eleven thousand companions proved faithful to their divine Spouse, even to the shedding of their blood. Now, the Holy Spirit who gave them sufficient constancy to suffer martyrdom will likewise impart to us the strength we need, and assuage by the unction of His grace, the austerities and trials He imposes on us in the Religious state. Who would fear, or be wanting in courage, having before her such holy examples and such powerful aids?

This reflection should induce us to embrace our Rules and Constitutions with love, and to practise them with fidelity, bearing in mind this great truth,—as Jesus has entered into His glory by the way of suffering and the Cross, and has traced for us a similar path, so it is by doing violence to ourselves in subjecting our whole being to God, and by surmounting the difficulties we experience in this practice. that we shall follow Him and merit the crown He has prepared for us.

✠

J. M. J. A. U. A.

THE RULE

OF

OUR FATHER, SAINT AUGUSTIN.

CHAPTER I.

OF THE END AND SPIRIT OF THE INSTITUTE.

First, my very dear Sisters, love God above all things; and secondly, your neighbor as yourselves: for these two commandments have been given to us principally.

CHAPTER II.

OF UNION AND MUTUAL CONFORMITY.

Then follow those things which we order to be observed in your Monastery. Remember, first, that the purpose for which you are assembled is to live in union and concord; that you may have but one heart and one soul in God.

CHAPTER III.

OF POVERTY.

Be careful not to have anything in particular, but all in common, and that food and clothing be distributed to every one of you, by your Superioress; not equally, for all have not equal need; but to each, according to her necessity. It is thus we read in the Acts of the Apostles, "*that all things were in common.*"

Let those who bring fortunes to the Monastery, willingly put them in common; but those who had none in the world, should not come to seek in the Monastery what they could not have had elsewhere. They must, however, be assisted in their infirmity, and their wants must be supplied, although in the world, their poverty might have been so great, that they could not procure even the necessaries of life. Let them not esteem themselves happy for having found in the Monastery the conveniences of diet and clothing, which they could not have had elsewhere; nor become vain at being associated with, and made companions of those whom they would not have presumed to approach in their former state; let them rather raise their hearts to Heaven and not amuse themselves in seeking terrestrial comforts lest it happen that the Monastery be profitable to the rich and not to the poor, if the rich are there made humble and the poor become proud.

Care must also be taken that those who held some rank in the world, should not despise their sisters who, having been poor, were received into this holy society. Let them endeavor to rejoice more in the company of their poor sisters, than at the dignity of their wealthy relatives. Neither should they exalt themselves if they have contributed of their means for the support of the Community, or esteem themselves the more for having given their fortune to the Monastery, than if they had continued to enjoy it in the world; for all sorts of sins appear in the accomplishment of bad works, but pride lies in wait for good deeds, to destroy them. To what purpose is it to give one's goods to the poor, and to become poor one's self, if the miserable soul become prouder in despising them, than she had been in possessing them? Live then together in perfect union and concord, and honor God, revering in each other, His sacred temples.

CHAPTER IV.

OF PRAYER.

Apply to prayer and meditation at the hours and time appointed. Let nothing be done in the oratory, or choir, but that for which it is destined. If, besides the hours prescribed, some having leisure, desire to pray there, they should not be prevented or disturbed by others.

When you are occupied in church service, that is, in reciting or singing the psalms or hymns, let your heart be attentive to what your voice pronounces.

CHAPTER V.

OF CHASTITY.

Subdue your flesh by fasting and abstinence as far as your health will permit. But, if some cannot do this strictly, they should, at all events, not take anything out of the usual hours of meals, unless they be sick.

When you come to table, be careful to listen quietly and attentively to the lecture which is read according to custom, in order that not only the mouth may receive its nourishment, but that the ear be also replenished with the word of God.

If some be treated differently from others, on account of the infirmities they have contracted by their former diet or manner of living, this should not appear unjust or unreasonable to those whose constitutions are more robust; nor should they esteem the infirm happier for getting better nourishment than they do; they should rather feel consolation at enjoying that good health which the others do not. If more clothing, food, bed-clothes, etc., be given to those who come to the Monastery after having been delicately reared in the world, than to others who are stronger and of course happier; those to whom these things are denied, should consider how much the former have relinquished of the life they led in the world, although they cannot attain to the frugality and abstinence of the latter who have more vigor. These must, therefore, not be displeased if more be given to such delicate persons, as this is not done to show them more respect, but to relieve their infirmity; otherwise a deplorable evil would ensue, that in the Monastery, where the rich are taught to labor as much as they are able, the poor should, on the other hand, become delicate.

Though it may be expedient to give but little food to the sick, for fear of overcharging their stomachs; yet, when recovering, they must be well treated so as speedily to regain their former strength even though they have arisen from the lowest condition of the poor, for they have fallen by their sickness into the same state of infirmity which the rich had from the beginning, because of their delicate rearing. However, when restored to health, they must return to their better and happier custom, which is more becoming the servants of God; nor must they, when in health, seek the indulgences that were necessary for them when sick. Let those who have strength to support frugality deem themselves happy, for it is more desirable to want little, than to have much.

Let no singularity appear in your dress, and seek, not to please by your apparel but by your conduct. Your hair must not be carefully arranged, nor at all exposed, nor flow negligently, but rather be covered by your head-dress.

Seek rather to be in the company of your sisters than alone, and let nothing appear, either in your walk, carriage, gestures or movements that could offend the eye of others, but all that gravity and modesty becoming the sanctity of your holy Profession; and keep so strict a watch over your eyes, as never to fix them on any person.

CHAPTER VI.

OF FRATERNAL CORRECTION AND RELIGIOUS HUMILITY.

Let not those who fail in their duty, seek to hide themselves from others, or remain satisfied, thinking no one sees them; for they are seen when they least expect it. Yet, even should they succeed in hiding themselves from creatures, what can they do to conceal themselves from that Eye from which nothing remains hidden? Dare we flatter ourselves that God does not behold us, because He views things all the more patiently as He considers them more wisely? Let the Religious, therefore, fear to displease Him, rather than seek to please creatures, and let the remembrance of His all-seeing Eye help her to overcome that inordinate desire or fear of being seen by others; for, on this subject, we recommend the fear of God.

If you remark, in any of your sisters, a considerable defect, inform her thereof without delay, that she may correct herself and prevent the evil from increasing. But, if, after having been warned, you see she relapses, you should denounce her as a sick person who requires to be cured, after having made one or two observe it, that, in case of necessity, she may be convicted by the testimony of two or three, and reproved with such severity as may be found expedient. Do not, however, look upon yourself as disaffected towards her, for if, by your silence you allow to perish your sisters whom you might have corrected by a timely discovery, you partake in their guilt. If your sister had a bodily wound which she wished to hide, fearing an incision, would it not be cruelty in you to conceal it, and charity, to discover it? How much more then, ought you to manifest her spiritual wound, lest a more dangerous corruption be engendered in her soul?

But, previous to her being brought before those by whom she is to be convicted, in case she denies the fact, she must first be brought to the Superioress and privately reprehended, so that few may be acquainted with her fault. But if she persists in denying it, the others must be called, that she may not only be tried before one witness, but convicted before all, by the testimony of two or three.

Being convicted, she must submit to the penance and chastisement of her fault, according to the decision and discretion of the Superioress or of the Superior-priest. If she refuses to receive it, she must be separated from the rest, (which is charity, not cruelty,) for fear of destroying them by her pestilential contagion; and in order that she herself, being confined in some cell or prison, and forbidden to enter the Choir, the Refectory, and the Recreation-room, may be better able to reflect on her conduct and to acknowledge her fault.

This same method must be carefully observed in the research, conviction and correction of all faults, but always with a great love of the persons and hatred of their vices.

If any one commit so great a fault as to receive letters or presents clandestinely and acknowledges it, of her own accord, she is to be pardoned and prayed for; but if she be detected and convicted, she ought to be punished severely, at the discretion of the Superioress, or as the Superior-priest, or even the Bishop shall judge proper.

CHAPTER VII.

OF CLOTHING AND CLEANLINESS.

Let your habits be kept in the same place, under the care of one or two, or as many as may be necessary, to keep them in good order and preserved from moths.

As your nourishment is supplied from the funds of the house, so should your clothing be likewise obtained from the same source.

Be not solicitous about the clothing given you; whether it be suited to the season or not, nor about what you have left off, or if it were worn by another, contenting yourselves that you are in want of nothing necessary. Should murmuring and contention arise on this head, so that any one complains of getting worse clothes than she had before, and that she does not deserve to be more indifferently clad than others, hereby you may judge how deficient you are in sanctity and in the interior ornaments of the soul, since such anxiety arises for those of the body.

When you get your habits, those you lay aside must be kept in a common wardrobe, and all must be under the charge of the same person, in order that no one may work in particular for herself, whether for the bed, habit or other clothing; but all should be done for the Community with more care and pleasure, than if it was for herself, for it is written that *"Charity seeketh not its own,"* and this is manifested by preferring common to particular works, and not particular works to common. In proportion as you find you pay more attention to what is common than to what is particular, you will perceive the progress you have made, and it will be evident that Charity which is permanent, holds the first place in your hearts and shines forth even in the use of casual necessaries.

Whatever persons from abroad may give to their daughters, relations or other inmates of the Monastery, whether it be clothing, or other necessaries,—must not be received clandestinely, but left in the power of the Superioress, that being put in common, all may be disposed of indiscriminately, as necessity may require. If it happens that any one conceals what has thus been given to her, she must be condemned as guilty of theft.

The habits you leave off at different seasons must be brushed and mended, either by yourselves or others, as the Superioress may direct; for possibly too great a desire of exterior neatness may produce interior stains in your souls.

CHAPTER VIII.

OF THE CARE OF THE SICK AND THE WANTS OF THE SISTERHOOD.

If any sick person requires assistance, it must not be deferred, but given without murmur, according to the advice of the physician. Though she should not even desire it, the Superioress must insist upon her doing what is expedient for her health; if, on the contrary, she should wish for what is hurtful, she must not be gratified, for we esteem all that pleases us, as salutary, though it be really prejudicial.

If the servant of God has any hidden corporal pain, she must be credited, nor should it be doubted that she suffers the indisposition of which she complains. However, in order to ascertain whether what she desires be expedient for the relief of her complaint, the physician must be consulted, when there is no other means of assurance.

One of the sisterhood must be appointed for the care of the sick, the infirm, or those who are in a state of convalesence, in order to obtain from the depository, what may be requisite for them.

Those who are charged with the depository, habits, shoes, books, etc., should cheerfully serve their sisters and not delay giving what is necessary.

CHAPTER IX.

OF PEACE AND RECONCILIATION.

Carefully avoid disputes and contentions; but, should they arise, terminate them speedily, lest anger become hatred, and a mote be thus increased to a beam. *"He who hates his brother is a murderer."* This sentence, though written for man as first created, extends likewise to woman.

Whoever offends her sister by harsh, injurious words, or by a reproach for some grave fault, should repair the evil by immediate satisfaction; and she who has been offended should forgive without contestation. If both be in fault and have given mutual offense, they should be reconciled and have recourse to prayer, which ought to be the more holy, as it is more frequent among you. She who, though often tempted to anger and quickness of temper, readily apologizes, is more praiseworthy than another who is not so easily moved, but reluctantly acknowledges her fault. Those who refuse to forgive should not expect that their prayers will be heard; and those who refuse to apologize or who do so against their will, are uselessly to themselves, in the Monastery.

Abstain therefore from all rude and uncivil words. But, should they escape your lips, be not remiss in applying a proper remedy from the same source whence the wound proceeded.

When it is necessary to make use of harsh expressions, either for the instruction or the reprehension of those confided to your care, and that on these occasions, you have exceeded the just bounds of moderation, you are not under pretence of humility to ask pardon of them for your fault, for this may diminish your authority, and render you less useful to them. Acknowledge it, however, to *the common Lord and Master of all*, who knows with what tenderness you love those whom you have perhaps reprehended with unnecessary warmth. Love should be spiritual and not sensible among you.

CHAPTER X.

OF OBEDIENCE AND THE OBSERVANCE OF THE RULE.

Obey your Superioress as your Mother, showing her the greatest respect, and still more carefully honor the Superior-priest who has the charge of you all.

In order that these injunctions may be punctually observed, and that nothing, through negligence, pass without correction or amendment, the Superioress will be particularly watchful; and if anything surpass her ability, she shall inform the Superior-priest who superintends you.

As to her, let her not esteem herself happy to have the power of governing and commanding, but rather to be enabled to serve her sisters with charity. Let her have precedence and honor before the world, but before God, let her keep herself humbly at your feet, and be to all an example of good works. She should correct the unruly, console the pusillanimous, support and cherish the infirm, be patient towards all—ready to correct when necessary, but imposing correction with fear. Let her seek rather to be loved than dreaded, though both are useful, remembering always, that she has to render an account of you to God. For this reason, in obeying her, compassionate not only yourselves, but others whose danger is to be all the more feared as their position is more exalted.

May God's grace enable you to observe these ordinances joyfully and with charity, loving the interior beauty of virtue, and by your example, to become *a good odour in Jesus Christ;* not as servants under the yoke of the Law, but as persons of free condition under the ordinance of grace.

But in order that you may see yourselves in this Rule, as in a mirror, let it be read once a week, lest through forgetfulness, you neglect anything. If you find you have done what is prescribed, thank God from whom all good proceeds. But if you perceive you have failed in any point thereof, repent of the same and be more careful in future, beseeching God to pardon your fault and to protect you from temptation.

LAUS DEO.

INTRODUCTION.

SHOWING THE NECESSITY OF COMBINING THE INTERIOR DISPOSITIONS OF SPIRIT AND GRACE, WITH THE EXTERIOR OBSERVANCE OF THE RULES.

"*The law was given by Moses, but grace and truth came by Jesus Christ.* (John i. 17). Thus speaks the beloved disciple who by these words makes the same distinction between the law and grace, between the figure and the reality, as there is between Moses, the minister and dispenser of the old Law, and Jesus Christ our Lord, the Author of the grace and truth of the New Testament; or, as St. Paul expresses it,— between the servant and laborer of the house, and its Master and architect;—between the servants and slaves, and the children and heirs of a family. "*For*," says the same Apostle, "*we have not received the spirit of servitude in fear, but the spirit of adoption of children of God, to whom we cry, Abba, Father.*" Now, if this grace and privilege is common to all the faithful, how much more does it belong to souls consecrated to God by sacred vows—to souls doubly Christian and religious, bound to Jesus by the character marked upon the soul in Baptism, and again by a second consecration in the profession of the Religious state. This argument applies in a special way to the Ursuline Religious of the Presentation of our Lady, who should be the daughters of beautiful love, as their cherished and honored Patroness, the admirable Virgin, is the *"Mother of beautiful love."* They should not rest beneath the shadow of the Mosaic Law, but in the truth of christian grace. They have not been called to this holy state, to serve God as slaves, in fear, but in love, as the children of God and the spouses of the Heavenly King. They are obliged to live and to act, not only according to the letter, but according to the vivifying spirit; because, *"the dead and inanimate flesh profiteth nothing. It is the spirit which quickeneth,"* and *the letter without the spirit, killeth, but "the spirit giveth life."* (John vi) Now, as in the creation of man, God united two substances,—the material body and the spiritual soul,—the body formed of the earth, and the soul which emanated from Heaven, and which gives life to the body, being the principle of its movements and operations: and as, in the order of grace, God has added the Gospel to the Law, reality to figures, and the spirit of Christianity to the Mosaic code,—so should we, in like manner, distinguish in each Community properly established,—the body and the soul,—the letter and the spirit. The body or the letter relates to exterior practices and observances of Rule, prescribed by the inspiration of the Spirit of Jesus who governs and directs His Church and the Religious Orders in His Church. But the soul,—the spirit which gives life and grace, is Jesus present, Jesus living, Jesus acting in souls by the power and plentitude of His spirit, by the efficacy of His grace, and by the sweetness of His love, which, as St. Paul says, *"is diffused into our hearts by the Holy Spirit who is given to us."*

Now, the connection and natural union that exists between our soul and our body, should serve as a type and model of the manner in which we should unite grace with practice,—the spirit with the letter, and interior dispositions with exterior observances, for our Lord does not count our actions; He weighs them; He considers our hearts rather than our hands, our love and not our gifts,—as it is said of Abel: "*The Lord had respect to Abel and to his offerings.*" (Gen. iv. 4). It is not laboring that will save us, but laboring well,—not praying, fasting, working,—but praying well, fasting well, working well: not observing religious discipline and the Rules, but observing them fervently and *well*, in the christian and religious sense of the word—that is to say, according to the spirit of our Lord Jesus Christ, with a pure intention, with love and holy interior dispositions, uniting and referring our actions as an homage to the most holy actions of Jesus and to the divine Spirit by which He was animated in all that He did while on earth. Thus His life will sanctify ours; His actions will infuse life and grace into ours; and our life, our time, and our actions will continually honor His; so that in our life, in our vocation, and in all our actions, we shall be as so many victims and living holocausts, immolated and consumed for His Glory and His love. May Jesus live in our mortal bodies, as the Apostle directs; that is to say, may he animate even the lowliness and weakness,—the corporal and external functions of our physical being. Glory to Jesus! for He is life in God; Glory to Jesus! for He is the source of life in our souls! Glory to Jesus! for He is our eternal life.

AMEN.

A. M. D. G.

CONSTITUTIONS

FOR THE

URSULINE RELIGIOUS

OF THE

PRESENTATION OF OUR LADY OF THE ORDER OF ST. AUGUSTIN.

PART I.

Treating of the Religious Vows and Virtues, and of other Exercises of Devotion.

CHAPTER I.

On the Charity towards God, Recommended in the Rule.

"*My dear Sisters, love God above all things, and then your neighbor as yourselves, for these two commandments have been given to us principally.*" In this, the first point of our Rule, our Father, St. Augustin, lays down as a foundation, the highest point of

Christian and religious perfection, which obliges us:—

1st. Never to consent to what we know to be contrary to the Commandments and the Will of God, or to what we have promised by our vows; and to detest sin above all things, because it extinguishes divine love in our hearts.

2d. To make frequent acts of love, animated by a deep reverence for the sovereign majesty and goodness of God; by the absolute preference we give Him above all things that are in Heaven or on earth; by a fervent and intimate union with Him, and by an unshaken constancy in His holy love—that thus we may be able to exclaim with the Apostle: "*Neither life, nor death, etc., nor any creature whatsoever, shall separate us from the love of God.*"

3d. To refer to God all that we do. "*Whether you eat or drink,*" says the same Apostle, "*do it for the glory of God.*" We should especially offer to Him our sufferings and anxieties, and consider Him as the principle and the end of all our actions.

INSTRUCTION.

To attain this pure and holy love of God, we must, in the first place, cost what it may, remove all obstacles thereunto. The principal of these obstacles is self-love; and as this has many branches, if it cannot be eradicated at one stroke, applying the axe to the root of the tree, let it, at least, be done little by little, and branch by branch; that is to say, let us cut off and renounce in detail and one by one, all affections and attachments to creatures and to ourselves; faithfully exercising ourselves each day in the practice of mortification and self-abnegation, if we desire to render ourselves worthy of Him who has said: "*If any one would be My disciple, let him renounce himself, take up his cross daily, and follow Me.*"

It does not suffice to root out the bad weeds; we must also plant good seed which will germinate and bring forth fruits of divine love. All the practices of the religious virtues, and the observance of the vows and Constitutions, are as so many means and steps towards the attainment of this virtue;

but the following are the principal among the dispositions to be cultivated:

1st. A great submission and conformity to the holy Will of God, desiring to accomplish it in all things, and begging that our Lord Jesus Christ would, in His goodness, deign at every moment of our life, to accomplish all His designs in our regard.

2d. Entertain a tender love and devotion towards the Sacred Humanity of Jesus, desiring to be clothed with Him, animated by His Spirit, and proposing the actions and virtues of His life to our imitation. Let this be our daily food and the most frequent subject of our converse with God during Meditation.

We should also have a sincere affection for the Blessed Virgin Mary, and a filial confidence in her intercession as the Immaculate Mother of God. We should, moreover, honor the Saints to whom we are under special obligations—particularly those who have been the objects of the predilection of Jesus and Mary. Among these, St. Mary Magdalen, the model of penitent love, should be regarded as the precious vase, and one of the fittest objects of the predilection of the Son of God, who, it may be believed, wished to repair in her at His feet the seraphic love that had been lost in Heaven.

Now, as she is not only a Daughter to receive, but also a Mother of this beautiful love, to impart and to spread it by her intercession, she should be invoked, to destroy self-love in our souls, and to share with us the plenitude of her love for Jesus, who said of her: "*She hath loved much.*"

CHAPTER II.

On Charity Towards our Neighbor and Perfect Union Among the Sisters.

All the Sisters should be one in Jesus Christ, by a union of minds and, as much as possible, of sentiments; as He is one with His Father by a unity of essence. They should be united among themselves by a conformity of will, as He is one with His Father in unity with the Holy Ghost. They should be united and bound together by a uniformity of rule, customs and usages, and (with the consent of the Ordinary) by a mutual communication of the temporal necessaries of life, as Jesus is one principle with the Father, in regard to all exterior things—that is to say, He is the same Creator and Ruler of the world. Thus the desire of Jesus will be accomplished in them: "*May they be one in us, as Thou, Father, and I are one.*"

It is said of the first Christians that they had but one heart and one soul; in like manner, all hearts in this Community should be united to the Heart of Jesus, and each will should be submissive to His.

To maintain this union, the Sisters must carefully banish from their Community all that could, in the least, disturb this spirit of peace, or break this holy bond of charity, namely: bitterness, words of reproach, and contention, which, according to the Apostle, indicate a sensual soul—that is, one filled with herself, and seeking her own interests rather than those of Jesus Christ.

2d. Injuries, insults, and other offensive actions, should not be tolerated without condign satisfaction.

3d. The Sisters must shun all intriguing assemblies, and all murmuring against the Superioress or the other officials of the House.

4th. Let nothing be permitted that could injure charity; such as murmurs, detractions, false reports—in a word, whatever might be prejudicial to the honor and reputation of others, whether in or out of the Monastery.

5th. Particular friendships and attachments, which are so many retrenchments from the affection and charity which are universally and equally due to all, to restrict them to a few, should be exterminated as the pest of Religious Communities.

INSTRUCTION.

"*God is Charity, and he who lives in Charity, lives in God,*" says the beloved Disciple. It is the special prerogative of this virtue, that God is its giver, its merit and its reward, its means and its end, since, being Charity itself, He is also its consummation. Now this virtue which unites us so intimately with God, unites us at the same time divinely among ourselves, thus producing in us the effects of the prayer which Jesus addressed to His Father: "*May they be one in us, as Thou, Father, and I are one.*" For the maintenance and increase of this union and mutual charity, there are three necessary dispositions suitable to the life and spirit of true Ursulines.

1st. A mutual deference towards one another, honoring and respecting each, according to the requirements of her position. They should see in each Sister the living image of God, and esteem her as a member united to Jesus and vivified by His grace; finally, let them honor in each the virtues and good qualities with which God has endowed her, and show her due respect as the much loved spouse of Jesus Christ. However, on this point, two extremes are to be avoided : first, that of treating one another with two much ceremony, and paying worldly compliments, after the manner of seculars; and, on the other hand, that of being too free and familiar, this being opposed to religious respect and modesty.

The second disposition consists in meekness, mildness and affability. Hence, the Sisters should try never to assume a frowning, severe, gloomy or haughty expression of countenance, but manifest in their exterior the gentleness, candor and interior joy of the soul; always answering mildly, and never using sharp, light or improper words in conversation, nor interrupting one another in difference of opinion; expressing their sentiment with sincerity and respect, but without violence or contestation.

The third disposition is patience and mutual forbearance of each other's humors and imperfections, according to this rule of the Apostle: "*Bear ye one another's burdens, and so you shall fulfil the law of Jesus Christ,*" for Charity is kind and patient—kind, never doing anything that could offend or give pain to others; patient, enduring whatever may be offensive or displeasing to ourselves. Religion is the holy school in which these virtues are to be learned, not only theoretically by study, but practically by their daily exercise.

This last disposition will help us to avoid and banish from the beginning all aversions and alienations which so easily insinuate themselves into minds, and which, once they have taken root, are so very difficult to eradicate. They ruin charity, trouble peace, and cause a thousand disorders in the interior and even in the exterior. Therefore, it is very important to foresee them, or to get rid of them from their first appearance.

CHAPTER III.

Formulæ for the Religious Profession and the Renewal of Vows.

In order that the Sisters may clearly understand what they promise in their Religious profession, and that they may have their obligations constantly present to their minds, we here give the formula of their Profession:—

"*I, Sister N., vow and promise to God, in honor of the ever Blessed Virgin Mary, of our Father, St. Augustin, our Foundress, St. Angela, our Patroness, St. Ursula, and of all the Saints: in your presence, my Lord, our Rt. Rev. Bishop and Superior,* (or, when the Bishop is not present) *in your presence, Rev. Father, as representing our Rt. Rev. Bishop and Superior; in yours, Rev. Mother, and that of the Community,*—POVERTY, CHASTITY *and* OBEDIENCE *until death, in this Religious Order of the Ursulines of the Presentation of our Blessed Lady, under the Rule* of our Father, St. Augustin, and in accordance with the Brief of our Holy Father, the Pope, and the approved Statutes and Constitutions.

"*In testimony of which, I have signed myself Sister N.*"

After the holy Sacrifice of the Mass, on the Feast of our B. Lady's Presentation in the Temple, all the Sisters will, one after another, renew their Vows in a loud and distinct voice, according to the following formula:

"*I, Sister N., renew to God, my vows of Poverty, Chastity and Obedience, with a desire of increasing each day in new fervor, and begging of God the grace to observe them faithfully until death.*"

INSTRUCTION

On the Obligation of the Vows and of the Religious Profession.

The Son of God, our divine Saviour, came on earth as the Light of the world and the Sun of Justice, to enlighten our darkness, to teach us the way of salvation, and to make known to us the wishes of God His Father.

He expresses some in the form of absolute commandments, to the observance of which He obliges us by the following words: "*If thou wilt enter into life, keep My commandments.*" Others are expressed in the form of a counsel or advice, inviting us to greater perfection, as when He says: "*If thou wilt be perfect, go, sell all thou hast and give to the poor, and come, follow Me.*" These latter are what we call the Evangelical Counsels, which are as so many means and paths to perfection. They are comprised in the three vows of Religion—voluntary Poverty, perpetual Chastity and Obedience, in the observance of which consists the state of Religion and of evangelical perfection.

These counsels, before being promised to God by the vows, are only recommended; but, after they have been vowed, they are absolutely commanded. Before the Religious Profession, they are voluntary and of devotion, but afterwards, they are necessary and of obligation, so much so, that the salvation of the soul and the perfection to which the Religious are bound to aspire, are, as it were, inseparably united. They cannot attain the one without aspiring to the other; and it might be said to them, "If you will enter into life, observe not only the commandments, but also the Counsels you have promised, and which hold for you the place of commandments." Moreover, according to these words of life: *"Unless you become as little children,"* that is to say, humble; unless you are poor, chaste and obedient, not only shall you not be perfect and holy, but *you shall not enter the Kingdom of Heaven;* for the infraction of the Religious Vows in a serious point is a sin which deprives the soul of grace and glory, just as sins against the commandments affect the rest of Christians.

The Profession which the Religious make embraces several points. The first, and apparently the principal, is the perpetual and irrevocable donation which the Religious makes of herself—her being, her entire substance, her body, her soul, her mind, her liberty, all her actions and every moment of her life and eternity—henceforth renouncing herself and all things else, in order to be all to God and to Him who died for her on the Cross. This donation, thus made on earth, is ratified and accepted in Heaven by God, in whose name it is received by the Order and the Superiors, who exercise the new right and power He has thereby acquired over the soul.

For this reason the Religious Profession is called a second Baptism; because, as in Baptism, the guilt of sin is forgiven and the punishment due to it entirely remitted, so does the Religious Profession produce a similar effect by the Plenary Indulgence which is gained in the form of a Jubilee. Moreover, the Religious Profession is, as it were, a second bond which unites and consecrates the soul anew to God after that of baptism, which regenerates her spiritually and renders her conformable to Jesus Christ dying and rising from the dead.

Consequently, as in Baptism, we promise fidelity to the Church and the Faith, and receive in our souls an ineffaceable mark of our subjection to Jesus Christ—so also does the Religious Profession involve a perpetual stability in Religion; and as those who deny the Faith professed in Baptism are called apostates of the Church, so, in like manner, do those who violate their Religious Profession commit a sin of apostacy against Religion according to these words of Life: *"No one putting his hand to the plough and looking back, is fit for the Kingdom of Heaven."* Jesus Christ forbids us to look back, to teach us that not only contrary effects, but even desires, are criminal; because, as Lot's wife, after having been saved from the burning of Sodom, was, by looking back, changed into a statue of salt—so those, who having renounced the world, look back upon what they have left and desire what is no longer permitted them, are changed, as it were, into statues of desires and covetousness, similar, in some respects, to those of the reprobate, which remain ineffectual and serve only to torment them the more.

Finally, the Religious Profession is a mutual contract by which the soul binds herself to God and God to the soul. This engagement will ever remain inviolable on the part of God, and should be the same on ours. If we are faithful in giving God what is so justly His due, He will also be faithful in rewarding us according to His promises.

CHAPTER IV.

On Poverty.

The Sisters shall possess nothing in private, and have nothing of their own on earth, so that no one may be able to say, "This pin is mine." For this end, they should detach their affections from all things of which they have only the use, and it will be doing them no injustice to make them exchange even the most necessary objects in their use. It is expedient to do this occasionally; as, for instance, to change their cells, habits, and other things, according to the prudence of the Mother Superioress, for fear that usage may imperceptibly hold the place of property.

The Sisters are not permitted to covet and claim the things they may have lawfully possessed before their profession; for, according to the Gospel: *"Any one putting his hand to the plough and looking back, is not worthy of the Kingdom of God."*

They should dispose of nothing whatsoever, nor receive from their own, or the boarders' parents, or from their friends and other persons, any gifts to claim for their private use; neither are they allowed to give anything whatsoever without the express permission of the Mother Superioress.—Whatever is thus given to a Sister by her parents or friends must be put in common, and she has no right to its use, unless the Superioress permits her to keep it; in which case she is allowed to use it for the time and in the manner the Rev. Mother may judge proper, and as a thing belonging to the Community.

The Sisters must never keep money for private use, under any pretext or license whatsoever. The Treasurer and the Housekeeper are charged with that of the House, and the Directress of the Academy keeps that of the children under her care. The Superioress may, with the advice of her Council, permit the Officials to keep money according to the necessities of their employments, but these must give her an account of it. Except in these cases, it is so expressly forbidden that (which may God forbid!) should a Sister after her death be found in possession of any hidden money which she had kept as her personal property she would be considered as excommunicated, and she could not be buried in consecrated ground.

Let the Sisters be careful not to lose, spoil, break, or misplace objects belonging to the Monastery—either wilfully or through carelessness; but endeavor to preserve everything as carefully as beggars keep what they have. Those who have charges must see that nothing is spoilt, wasted, or badly used in the employments.

The Sisters must shun all luxury and superfluity in their dress, as well as in their furniture—such as articles made of silk or silver, unless it be for the Church, the Oratories and the Sacristy. The forks and spoons for the use of the sick may be of silver, for the sake of greater cleanliness.

They shall have no box or anything else locked, except with the express permission of the Superioress; neither are they allowed to have books without the same permission; and, even then, they must mark them only with the inscription of the Monastery.

As the Mother Superioress should be very careful to provide with great charity for each one's necessities, so all should be satisfied with the common usage in regard to food, clothing, and lodging, and with what suffices for the poverty of the Religious State and of the Servants of Jesus Christ; preserving the greatest possible equality, and never seeking any singularity or privilege, except what the necessities of infirmity or old age may require.

INSTRUCTION.

Poverty is a royal virtue, since the Kingdom of Heaven belongs to the poor; and it has been made divine in the person of Jesus Christ, the King of kings, who has taught it by His example—being born in a stable and living poor in the world. He has also taught it by word, preaching it to His Apostles in His Sermon on the Mount: *"Blessed are the poor in spirit,"* (Matth. v.) establishing it as the foundation of the lofty tower of evangelical perfection, and promising, besides a hundredfold in this life, a treasure in the next, to those who will have left all to follow Him. In accordance with these lessons and promises, the true Daughters of St. Ursula should courageously embrace holy Poverty; cherish and love it tenderly—and preserve it with a holy jealousy, in order to render themselves worthy to follow our Lord, to imitate His example, and to obey His precepts.

Now, in order to embrace holy Poverty with more exactness and perfection, the Profession which the Sisters make invites them (1) to despise the goods of the earth and to prize them no more than clay; for our Saviour says: "*Where your treasure is, there also should be your heart*"—that is to say, in Heaven and in the Heart of your divine Spouse.

(2). To seek for, and choose for their private use, the poorest and meanest articles, whether in clothing, food, furniture, or other things.

(3). To be poor, not only in not having or possessing anything, but also in willingly enduring the want or privation of things that seem necessary; for it is very easy to be poor, provided nothing be wanting to us. The perfection of Poverty consists in bearing indigence and rejoicing in want, after the example of Him who became poor for us, in order to enrich us by His poverty.

Lastly, the Sisters should confide all things to the holy and paternal Providence of God, withdrawing all care and solicitude from temporal things; for He is a good Father who knows our wants. It is He who feeds the birds of the air; He loves with a paternal love those who abandon themselves to Him, and He will never permit them to be in want of the necessaries of life.

CHAPTER V.

On Chastity.

As the exterior senses are the doors by which death and sin enter the soul, the Sisters must be very careful never to expose them to bad, unlawful, dangerous, or even curious objects that might become an occasion of evil imaginations either in themselves or others. Let them study to mortify their hearing, taste, smell and touch—but above all, their sight, this being very severely recommended by our Father, St. Augustin, in his Rule. In fine, they should not permit a day to pass without some acts of mortification of the senses. They should never keep a profane picture, or even one of devotion, if immodest or unbecomingly nude.

They must guard themselves against particular friendships and improper familiarity with the other Sisters, as also against secret conversations, especially during the hours of silence, and without permission.

Each one must sleep apart, and not two together; but the Superioress may permit, not only the sick and infirm, but also the young and timorous, to sleep together in a large room or infirmary—each one, however, in her own bed.

They must not allow their hair to grow to any length, nor let it be seen; and should have it cut at least twice a year.

All that could excite sensuality—for instance, musk, perfumes, and other luxuries—must be banished from the Monastery, except when required for the sick. Profane songs, and all kinds of delicacies and curiosities in dress or person, must be avoided as inimical to true Chastity.

The Sisters shall not wear rings, gloves,

or silk; each one making it her chief care and endeavor to become, as the Apostle says: "*Holy in body and in mind, and to bear in her body the mortification of Jesus Christ.*"

INSTRUCTION.

"*Chaste souls are temples of the Holy Ghost, and pure bodies are the members of Jesus Christ,*" says the Great Apostle. Chastity gives us two kinds of relations with these Divine Persons, consecrating our souls to the Holy Ghost as His living temples, and uniting our bodies to Jesus Christ as members to their head.

These two Divine Persons can be, and are given only, to purity. Thus, the Son of God was given by His Father to the Blessed Mary, who is the purest among virgins and the most chaste of mothers; and the Holy Ghost, who is the Gift of the Father and the Son, communicates Himself only to pure souls.

The Sisters should, therefore, love this angelic virtue, which makes them the Spouses of the King of Angels, and prepares in their hearts a dwelling for the Holy Ghost. To this they are exhorted by the Apostle, who says: *"I beg of you, by the mercy of God, that you present your bodies as living, holy, and agreeable victims."*

As this evangelical Pearl must be sought with care, and preserved at any cost, even, if necessary, at that of life itself—the Religious of St. Ursula, who make a special profession of this virtue, must endeavor to preserve a strong desire of purity, both of mind and body, not only in themselves, but also in the young girls under their charge—taking all possible care and precaution to be chaste in thought and in affection, which they should keep entirely for their Heavenly Spouse—never engaging or attaching themselves to any object except Himself.

There are three faithful guardians of purity, namely: Mortification of the body, true humility of mind, and a special devotion to the Sacred Humanity of Jesus and to His Immaculate Mother,—loving and honoring their ineffable purity, and begging to receive from them a share in this virtue.

CHAPTER VI.

On Obedience.

Good Religious should be persuaded that they no longer belong to themselves, and should no longer live for themselves, but that they belong to and should live for Him alone, who has redeemed them by His death, and to whom they have consecrated themselves. Hence, it is no longer in their power, nor are they free to dispose of their person, their time, their actions, their employments, and other things; all of which must be left to the will of their Superioress, whom they should obey as our Lord Himself, were He visibly on earth. As the contract was in the beginning voluntary, but subsequently became binding, so that which was heretofore a vow of simple devotion has since the Profession become a matter of precise obligation. Hence, let no one undertake anything, nor interfere in any affairs, or in the offices of the other Sisters, nor do anything of importance, receive or send letters or messages, without the permission of the Superioress, to whom,—or to the one appointed by her,—all letters must be brought for inspection.

Should it happen that the Superioress commands things that seem difficult or impossible, the Sisters may, with mildness and submission, once, and with permission, even twice, give their reasons. But, if the Superioress, having well understood them, still persists in her command, the Sisters must yield and obey without further reply, at once mortifying their own judgment, and believing that it is the will of God, Who will give them grace and strength to accomplish what is ordained.

They should not go into each other's rooms to remain there for a considerable time, nor into the Infirmary or the office-rooms, without permission or necessity.

Each Sister should be prompt and exact in repairing to the observances and assemblies of the Community, that the others may not be obliged to wait for her. Hence, at the sound of the bell, she should punctually leave her work, reading, or any other occupation in which she may be engaged, to go where Obedience summons her.

Each Sister should receive with submission and as coming from our Lord the office that is assigned her, trying to perform it with great care, exactitude and fidelity, so that nothing may be wanting on her part, and that all may be done at the time, in the place and in the manner prescribed. The Sisters should also obey each one in whatever concerns her office—that is to say, the Sacristan in what regards her charge, the Infirmarian in the Infirmary, the Directress of the Choir in her office, and so on the others. When there are several in the same employment, there must be a Superintendent whom the rest should obey.

The Sisters shall make no humiliation in public, nor perform any private penance or mortification, without having obtained permission.

Let nothing be considered trivial in the customs and ceremonies, for in the House of God all should be weighed in the scales of the Sanctuary; for this reason they must be studied with care.

All that takes place in the interior, as well as in the exterior, should be regulated by obedience. For this end the Novices should manifest their interior to their Mistress once a week; and the Sisters should once a month do the same to the Superioress, or, with her permission, to the Assistant. This will be done with profit and advancement, if the Superioress shows them a maternal heart, and receives them with meekness and affability. The Sisters should have recourse to her with entire confidence, manifesting all their necessities, corporal as well as spiritual—candidly acquainting her with their interior, without concealing any of their devotions or sentiments—in order that she may have the entire disposal of their person; remembering that there is no sacrifice more pleasing to God than that of our own will and liberty.

INSTRUCTION.

God governs all things in the order of nature and of grace by the laws of obedience. Our nature and our being are essentially slaves to the sovereignty of God. Even His highest Creatures — His Angels — are called His Servants, doing His will. But, to deify this virtue, He wished His only Son, Jesus Christ, to be capable of obedience and submission in our nature, and to become obedient unto death, even to the death of the Cross; so that by constant submission to the will of His Eternal Father, from the first instant of His life to the very last, He should rather lose His life than disobey Him. Therefore, as by the disobedience of the first man we were all lost, so by the obedience of Jesus Christ we are all sanctified. Behold here a powerful motive to follow Jesus on the road traced by obedience. This virtue should be the prime mover of Religion, and direct all other virtues and actions.

The vow of Obedience made in the Religious Profession brings with it so great a blessing on the whole life, that all which is afterwards done in accordance with the Rules and the ordinances of our Superiors merits eternal life, in virtue of this first sacrifice, although it may be done without reflection.

The object of Obedience should not be a mortal person, the Superioress for instance, but God Himself and Jesus our Lord, whom we ought to revere in her person; for He said to the chiefs and rulers of His Church: "*He that heareth you, heareth Me; and he that despiseth you, despiseth Me.*" Hence, we should consider, not so much the talents or natural defects, the grace, virtue or faults of a Superioress, but rather the divine authority and the power she has received from God over souls. As the Israelites were led and directed by the Ark which, though inanimate, represented the Majesty of God,—so, were we commanded to obey the trunk of a tree, in it we should revere the authority of God—willingly subjecting ourselves to others for God's sake.

The perfection of Obedience consists in not only doing what is commanded, but in submitting our own will and renouncing our own judgment. Hence, perfect Obedience requires the following dispositions:

(1). It must be prompt and exact, performing with diligence and exactitude what the Rule or the Superioress ordains.

(2). It must be humble, without complaint—surmounting repugnances and contradictions.

(3). It must be simple—avoiding replies, excuses and arguments, which frequently destroy the merit of Obedience.

(4). It must be pure and sincere—obeying the Superioress, not for any human motive or interest, but only because she represents the person of our Lord Jesus Christ.

(5). It must be filial and cordial—that is to say, proceeding from childlike love, and not servile, like that of slaves who obey through fear of punishment. For this end we should love the Superioress with a pure and truly spiritual love, and esteem what she commands.

CHAPTER VII.

Retreat and Solitude.

As the Spouse in the Canticles is twice called by her Beloved a closed garden, we may infer that there are two kinds of solitude: the one interior, and the other exterior. The first regards ourselves; the second, others. The seclusion or enclosure of the Monastery, without interior recollection of mind, would be more like a prison than a religious retreat.

The Sisters shall annually take the time appointed for them to make a retreat of eight days, in order to repair the faults of the past year by an annual Confession, to renew themselves in the spirit of their vocation by a renovation of their dispositions, and to gain the Indulgences accorded by the Holy Father. This retreat should be made in honor and in imitation of the Blessed Virgin and the Apostles, who, during ten days, persevered with her in prayer, to dispose themselves to receive the Holy Ghost. No one is allowed to dispense herself from these Exercises; but the Mother Superioress may, with the sanction of the Director, abridge the time, or dispense those she thinks unable to bear this solitude, on account of their infirmities, or for other reasons. This dispensation should, however, be given as rarely as possible.

The Sisters are also advised to take in each month a day of recollection; for instance, the feast of their monthly Patron, or any other day, according to their devotion.

There must daily be an hour for retreat, namely: from 11 to 12 o'clock, which is to be employed in saying the Litany of the Blessed Virgin, making the Particular Examination, saying the Beads and the Litany of the Saints, with only the last "Prayer" for the living and the dead. After this, each Sister may read or employ herself according to her devotion.

The Sisters should preserve a greater recollection during the three days of Tenebræ, during Lent, and on all fast days. On the solemn festivals of our Lord and the Blessed Virgin they should endeavor to be more interior than at other times, and their conversation, like that of the Apostle, should be in Heaven.

They will have no recreation on Friday evenings, which are to be spent in recollection, in honor of our Saviour's Passion, and His silence and solitude during the last night of His Mortal life. When a feast falls on Friday, the silence and recollection are to be observed on the eve.

INSTRUCTION.

Our true retreat and solitude is to be with Jesus our Saviour, and to abide with Him; and our dissipation is to be with ourselves. He is our centre, and the more we seek ourselves, the more do we withdraw from Him. "Lord, Thou hast made us for Thyself," said our Father, St. Augustin, "and our hearts are in a state of continual uneasiness until they return to Thee." Hence, the soul that is united to God by grace and charity, and submissive to Him by interior resignation— the soul who is one in spirit with God by adherence, according to these words of the Apostle : *"He who adheres to God forms but one spirit with Him"*—finds her solitude even in conversation, her rest in labor, and her retirement in the occupations of her charge; because, wherever the soul finds God, she finds in Him her centre, her repose and her solitude.

This interior recollection and solitude with the divine Spouse should be the perpetual banquet of souls consecrated to God; and, in order to foster it, the Sisters should, throughout the day, carefully preserve the spirit of prayer, which is their daily food, performing all their actions, even such as are most trivial in their employments and offices, as far as they are able, according to this principle. The following means will greatly assist them in acquiring this interior spirit:

(1). To choose, every day in morning Meditation, the point of the Mystery, or the disposition and affection which has most forcibly impressed the soul, to serve as a subject for recollection and interior elevation, amidst the diversity of daily occupations.

(2). Never to pass an hour without raising their hearts to God.

(3). Never to give or apply themselves to exterior occupations with such eagerness as would prevent them from endeavoring, like St. Catherine of Sienna, to form an oratory in their hearts, so that from time to time they may enter therein alone with Jesus, and converse with Him alone.

CHAPTER VIII.

The Time of Silence and the Hour of Retreat.

Silence causes the true religious spirit to flourish in Monasteries; hence, the Sisters should observe it strictly, and bear in mind that the time and the places in which it is prescribed require that they be more especially recollected, and in the disposition of the Prophet, who said: "*I will listen to what the Lord will say within me.*"

The most perfect silence is to be observed from the evening examination until Divine Office, which is said after the morning Meditation. During this interval it is not permitted to speak to one another without great necessity; and even in this case it should be done in a low voice, briefly, and in a retired place, so as not to be heard, and that the other Sisters' recollection may not be disturbed. Nevertheless, the Sisters are, at all times, permitted to speak, through necessity, to the Superioress, and the Novices to their Mistress, provided it be done in the manner above prescribed. The Sisters who have charge of the boarders during these hours must keep and cause silence to be kept as perfectly as circumstances will permit.

The Religious must observe silence in the Refectory, from the *Benedicite* of the meals until after the *Grace* at the first, as well as at the second table; as also in the Choir, Sacristy, Chapter-room, and in the Hall between the cells.

On Sundays and festivals the Sisters

should carefully employ their time in spiritual reading, prayer, and other holy exercises—never straying about the House without occupation. They may, however, take a half hour's relaxation after Vespers.

INSTRUCTION.

The highest and most worthy homage that can be offered to God is silence—by which the Angels and Saints incessantly praise Him in Heaven. Jesus our Lord, and His Blessed Mother, have given us an example of this virtue, for the evangelist records only four occasions when this pure Virgin spoke—once to the Archangel, once to her cousin Elizabeth, and twice to her divine Son; and Jesus, who is the Word of the Father, kept a profound silence during the whole time of His Infancy and during the night of His Passion. We should, therefore, honor the Silence of Heaven and imitate that of Jesus and Mary by our own. "*He is perfect*," says the Apostle St. James, "*who sins not by the tongue.*" As nothing more effectually destroys the interior spirit than too much talk, or a superfluity of words, so is silence its most faithful guardian. Alas! who would not fear to speak too much, when we hear our Saviour declare that "Man shall have to give an account of every idle word on the day of judgment.

It would, however, avail but little to keep silence exteriorly, if the soul cease not to speak within herself and to entertain herself with every trifle—to have her mind constantly agitated, distracted, and full of curiosity, superfluous care and solicitude, vexations, repugnances and private opinions. If, then, exterior silence is necessary for the good order of the Monastery, and to preserve the spirit of recollection in the Community—interior silence is indispensable for peace and tranquillity of soul. We must, therefore, acquire it:

(1). By retrenching and mortifying all superfluous desires, all affection and attachment towards anything whatever; by an indifference of our will and true death of the soul in regard to all things, because what we desire and love to excess fills and preoccupies our mind.

(2). By banishing all useless anxieties,

avoiding all curiosity in regard to things that do not concern us—in a word, all of which God will not ask us an account on the day of judgment.

(3). By being humbly and respectfully attentive to God, to His attractions and inspirations, for we must listen, rather than converse with Him, in accordance with these words of the Psalmist: *"I shall listen to what the Lord will say within me."* Finally, we should always be in the disposition of Samuel, when he said: *"Speak Lord, Thy servant heareth."*

CHAPTER IX.

Penances, Abstinence and Mortification.

Besides the fasts of obligation, which must be faithfully observed, the Sisters should fast every Friday in the year except from Easter to Ascension and during the octave of Christmas.

When it happens that a feast kept by the Church falls on Friday, the fast is transferred to Saturday, and if this is also a feast, the fast is to be omitted; as, also, when Thursday or Saturday are fast days, the Sisters shall not observe that of Friday. The same rule applies to days of abstinence that are immediately preceded or followed by a fast day.

The Sisters should also fast on the eve of the Ascension, that of Corpus Christi, and on those of all the feasts which are celebrated by the people in honor of the Blessed Virgin; the eve of her Presentation in the Temple, the eve of St. Ursula, and of our Father, St. Augustin.

On Good Friday only soup and a dish of vegetables or prunes should be served at dinner.

All the Wednesdays of Advent and those of Septuagesima and Sexagesima are days of abstinence. On these, and on all days of simple abstinence, only one dish should be served at the evening meal.

Although the Superioress should be strictly exact in having the fasts and abstinences observed in the Community, never granting an entire dispensation, let her, nevertheless, prove herself a kind and charitable Mother towards individuals—taking into consideration their infirmities, weakness, labor, and age, in order to dispense them without scruple, when, before God, she thinks proper to do so; and this especially with regard to those fasts which are prescribed by the Constitutions.

On all Fridays in the year, except during the octaves of Christmas and Easter, the exercise of the discipline is to be taken by all the Sisters in common during the time of a "*De Profundis,*" the versicle "*Christus factus est,*" etc., and the prayer, "*Respice quæsumus,*" etc. When it happens that a feast which has its vigil falls on a Friday this practice is to be performed on the eve, as also on the three days of Tenebræ and when a Sister dies in the Monastery. For those of other Houses of the same Congregation the Sisters shall add a "*De Profundis*" the first Friday after they have received the information. The Reverend Mother may propose the same exercise on Wednesday in Lent to those who may desire to perform it. The same may be done in public necessities; but in these cases those who so wish must take it in private.

There is to be in the Refectory a table called the "Table of the Poor," long enough to accommodate six (more or less) according to the number of Sisters. No tablecloth is to be put on this table, but only a napkin for each one, and bread staler than that served to the Community; and those who dine here are to use wooden forks and spoons. This table should be set every Monday, Wednesday, Friday and Saturday, except when a feast falls on any of these days, and on all vigils and fast days, so that each Sister may, with permission, dine thereat once a week. This practice is not obligatory, but should be performed to honor the poverty of Jesus, and with a desire to be treated as poor persons and beggars in His House. Nevertheless, the abstinence or dissimilarity of food at this table should consist in the quality rather than in the quantity.

On the eves of great festivals some of the Sisters may, through devotion and with the permission of the Superioress, perform humiliations in the Refectory. The same should be done by each Sister at the end of the annual Retreat. Having humbly accused herself of her faults, she must accomplish the penance imposed—as ordinarily, to kiss all the Sisters' feet—or any other, which should be done with great modesty and interior humiliation. Moreover, in the accusation, as well as in the imposition of penances, the Sisters should neither say nor do anything ridiculous or unbecoming to Religious humility. That these practices may be the more profitable, the Mother Superioress should permit them but rarely to each Sister.

The Sisters should often ask to perform some penance and mortification, either in private or in public, for the sake of edification. The Superioress should not readily grant permission, unless she sees a true desire and genuine dispositions. Let her permit humiliating practices, rather than bodily austerities.

INSTRUCTION.

Acts of penance performed without the spirit and the proper interior disposition are as a body without a soul, an instrument of music without sound or harmony, and as crosses devoid of unction and grace. St.

Mary Magdalen, the blessed lover of Jesus and the model of true penance, prostrated herself at the sacred feet of her Lord, and, bathing them with her tears, ceased not to kiss them. These two actions suggest to us the principal motives, and the two most excellent works of penance.

On the one hand, the sins and irregularities of our past life should pierce our hearts with lively sorrow and cause us, with this Saint, to shed tears of blood. On the other hand, the Goodness, the Love, and the Holiness of Jesus should inspire us with an ardent love of God above all things; and as sin should be to us a motive of sorrow, so should the essential Goodness of God be an incentive to love. Now, in imitation of this holy Lover and Penitent, who through these two motives was impelled to undergo a frightful solitude in retirement from the world—we should make religious penance consist chiefly in an eternal separation and divorce from the world and all its vanities—the very thought of which should be as so many thorns, the sight or presence, a torment—and even the necessary communication with it, a kind of martyrdom which we must suffer through necessity. Hence, the parlors and visits from seculars should be objects of real mortification.

All penances should be accompanied, as much as possible, with three principal interior dispositions: (1) Profound humiliation before the Majesty of God at the sight of our nothingness and our sins; (2) compunction or contrition of heart at the thought of God's Goodness and our ingratitude; and (3) ardent zeal to satisfy the justice of God and to avenge on ourselves the injury we have done Him by our transgressions. In these three dispositions is comprised the true spirit of penance.

Nevertheless, the desires of penance should always exceed the effects, and the effects should augment the desires—thus there will be no excess by indiscretion nor neglect through indifference and tepidity.

One of the most useful and salutary of penances is the cross which our Lord chooses and permits to fall to each soul, either as a mild and paternal correction of her faults or to purify and enable her to advance in the path of virtue. The same may be said of the daily mortifications that happen accidentally and unintentionally from the diversity of characters and from various other causes. The Cross of Jesus is, as it were, the source of crosses in chosen souls; hence, the Sisters should offer themselves generously and courageously to Jesus Crucified—each one receiving her cross, be it exterior or interior, as a heavenly manna—bearing it with humility, patience, and with the joy and peace of the Holy Ghost. Let them communicate it, however, with confidence to the Superioress, and dispose themselves for occasions of mortification, saying, with the Psalmist: "*It is a good thing that Thou hast humbled me.*"

The sacrifices of penance most agreeable to God are:

(1). The mortification of the body and the senses; (2) the renunciation of our own will and inclinations, and (3) the abnegation of our judgment and opinions. These are the three nails that must keep a true Religious fastened to the Cross of her Saviour, Jesus. Hence, all must be careful to exercise themselves in these three points—never permitting a day to pass without making some practices thereof.

We have, indeed, a very powerful incentive to do penance, when we consider that it is the only way that leads to Heaven, and we know of no Saint now in glory who did not perform great and austere penance during life. On the other hand, there is not one soul in hell who is not there because of the neglect of penance. After all, Jesus Crucified should be our chief model—for those who share His sufferings, shall likewise share His glory.

CHAPTER X.

Humility.

This virtue should be practised at all times, in all places, in every charge, under all circumstances, and with all persons, whether superiors or inferiors—honoring in all the gifts of God, although these are often hidden beneath the imperfections of human nature. The Sisters should never address one another by such titles as "*Lady*," "*Madam*," or "*Reverend*." The Superioress is to be called *Mother* only during the time of her superiority, as also the Assistant while she exercises her charge. The novices shall address their Mistress as *Mother*; but, in speaking of her, let them say "*Our Mistress.*" All the others are to be called *Sister*. Should any one be addressed as *Mother* by another Sister, she herself must kindly warn her not to give her that title; and in case this is continued, the Sister Zelatrice should warn the Community in general.

The Sisters should manifest towards one another a mutual and cordial respect; not, however, with worldly ceremonies and compliments, but with religious modesty and simplicity, especially towards the elder members and those who have been Superiors.

The Mother Superioress shall every where hold the first rank, and after her the Mother Assistant. Among the other professed members of the Chapter there is no right of precedence at any of the assemblies, except in Choir and at Chapter, where each is to take her rank of Profession.

When the Superioress reproves a Sister for any fault the latter shall kneel to receive the correction, unless prevented, and she must not rise until the Superioress bids her do so. Should she have something to say to justify herself, let her ask permission, and then speak with modesty and sincerity.

Should any contention arise in the Community between the Sisters, or should harsh, rude, injurious, or bitter words have been employed, the guilty should, at the slightest warning of the Superioress or the presiding Sister, humble themselves profoundly and ask pardon; after which, they should not say another word against each other. She who considers herself the most offended should be the first to humble herself, this proving her to be in the right.

As humiliations are the road to humility, the Sisters should endeavor to practise this virtue on all occasions, never permitting a single day to pass without performing some act of exterior or interior humiliation. They should willingly occupy themselves in work that seems most servile and abject; for instance, washing the dishes, helping in the laundry, and other employments of the Lay Sisters, whenever the Superioress permits or commands them to do so. This should, however, always be done with prudence, so that their health be not impaired. Before commencing these practices the Sisters should pay homage to the humiliations of the Son of God by some short prayer, remembering that little things done with great love and devotion are more agreeable to God than great and heroic deeds that proceed from a cold heart and are not accompanied with interior dispositions.

INSTRUCTION.

Religion is a school of deep humility; and the Religious life should be a constant practice of this virtue. Our Lord Jesus is its Sovereign Master and Doctor, for He has taught it by word and example, constantly reminding us of this beautiful lesson: *"Learn of Me, because I am meek and humble of Heart."* Whom shall we believe, if not Truth itself, and whom shall we follow, if not this Sovereign Pastor of our souls?

As pride, which precipitated Lucifer from Heaven, is the root and beginning of all sin and rebellion against God, and the certain sign of the reprobation of a soul, so it is humility that opens for us the gates of Heaven, according to these words of Life: *"Unless you become as little children you shall not enter the Kingdom of Heaven."* (Matth. 18.) Humility is the solid foundation of our salvation and of all virtue, and the most certain mark of predestination.

This virtue, above all others, must have its root in the inmost recesses of the heart and mind, producing at the same time visible fruits by the practice of exterior humiliations. Hence, a true Religious should always sincerely consider and believe herself to be the least among the Sisters, esteeming herself unworthy of being the servant of the others in the House of God, desiring to be treated in this quality, even as a sinner—to be despised and slighted by all; and when an occasion of contempt and self-abasement presents itself, she should embrace it with gratitude, and receive it as a precious manna which God has caused to fall from Heaven.

Moreover, as the life of Jesus, prefigured by His seamless garment, was one of continual humiliations, our Father, St. Augustin, teaches, that the first degree of the Christian life, or of perfection, is humility; the second is humility, and the third is humility. Hence, our duty is to humble ourselves all our life—and our Lord's office is to exalt us, in accordance with His word of truth: *"He that humbleth himself shall be exalted, and he that exalteth himself shall be humbled."* If now we usurp His office by exalting ourselves, He will take ours, which is to humble us forever. Alas! how terrible will be the punishment of the soul condemned on account of her pride!

CHAPTER XI.

On Piety, and the Exercises it Ordains.

The spirit of piety and devotion should be the prime mover of the life and actions of a Religious. The Sisters should, therefore, apply themselves to honor in a special manner all the mysteries of our holy Religion, according to the order and the dispositions of piety suggested to them. The devout custom of distributing the monthly Patrons on the first day of each month, and that of performing some devotions in their honor on the day of their feast, should be strictly observed. On the feast of the Ascension the Sisters shall draw cards of the mysteries of our divine Saviour's life; on Pentecost, the Gifts and Fruits of the Holy Ghost; on the feast of St. Michael, the nine choirs of Angels; and on that of our Blessed Lady's Presentation, her virtues.

The anniversary of the Vesture and Profession should be spent by each Sister in a Spiritual Retreat, to return thanks for the great mercy God has manifested towards her in her holy vocation, and to renew her spirit of fervor.

The Examination of Conscience shall be made twice a day, during about seven minutes. The first, before dinner, on the defects contrary to perfection, in order to renew the spirit of fervor; the second, at eight o'clock in the evening, on the faults against conscience, by way of humiliation and contrition.

The Sisters should daily offer some prayers—for instance, the Litany of the Saints—for the necessities of the Church, for the Holy Father, for the Bishop, and the State and city in which they live. In times of necessity, plague, war, or famine, they should redouble their devotions, visit the different Oratories within the Monastery, recite the Litanies, take the discipline, and perform other works of piety, to implore the Mercy of God.

They must daily say the Beads in private. As Spiritual Reading serves as food and nourishment to the spirit of piety, all the Sisters should make or hear some pious reading every day. They should listen to the Word of God with special attention and reverence, receiving it in the Conference, sermons and exhortations, with a desire to draw great profit therefrom, and as if it had been announced by the august lips of Jesus Himself.

INSTRUCTION.

Piety which makes us love and revere God and Jesus, our Saviour, as a tender Father, and which inspires us with a filial and reverential affection towards God, ought to be the life and soul of Religion. A Religious without devotion is as a trunk separated from its roots—as a body without a soul, and a lamp without light. As God formerly ordained that the sacred fire should be kept constantly burning in His Tabernacle, as a figure, so should we never allow the sacred fire of religious fervor and holy love to be extinguished on the Altar of our hearts.

Though a Religious were to forsake and renounce all the goods of this world; were she to possess the language and sentiments of an angel; were she to perform the greatest austerities, and even deliver her body to the flames—if all this were not animated by the spirit of piety and devotion; if she were devoid of love and charity—all this would be as nothing and of no avail for eternal life. She would be, according to the doctrine of the Apostle, *"as sounding brass and tinkling cymbals*" (Cor. 13). This disposition should be frequently recommended, since it alone gives strength, vigor and life to all the religious actions, virtues and observances. Without it retreat would be a prison, penance a torture, and this life a perpetual exile. On the other hand, the unction of divine love and of piety will render the yoke of our Saviour sweet and His burden light, and thus enable us to run joyfully in the way of His Commandments and Counsels.

The interior exercises of piety and devotion which the Ursulines, as Christians and Religious, should embrace are: (1) A profound submission to, and adoration of, the most adorable Trinity; (2) a humble and fervent devotion to Jesus our Saviour—to His Sacred Humanity and all the different states and mysteries of His life—honoring them according to the spirit of the Church at different seasons of the year: thus, in Advent, the mystery of His Incarnation and His nine months' abode in Mary's virginal womb; from Christmas until the Purification, His Birth and amiable Infancy; from the Purification until Lent,

His hidden life of thirty years; in Lent, the three years of His active Ministry, which the Church records in the Gospels; from Passion Sunday until Easter, His suffering Life, and so on, according to the mysteries that are celebrated:—His glorious Life in His Ressurrection, His celestial Life in His Ascension, the grandeur of the Holy Ghost in His Coming, and the wonders of the Hidden Life of Jesus in the adorable Sacrament of our Altars; finally, from the octave of Corpus Christi, until Advent, the ineffable grandeurs of Jesus in His Divinity and Humanity.

But of all the mysteries, there are two which should be held in special veneration in the Community, namely: the Sacred Infancy and the dolorous Passion of our divine Lord. Let the Sisters also have a tender, humble and loving devotion (1) towards the most Blessed Virgin, the dear Patroness, Mother and Lady of this Order which is particularly dedicated to her; (2) towards all the Saints of Jesus and Mary— that is to say, all those who were specially beloved by them, namely: St. Joseph, St. John the Baptist, St. Mary Magdalen, St.

John the Evangelist, and the other Apostles, besides other Saints of different periods; (3) towards the two Archangels, Sts. Michael and Gabriel, and the holy Guardian Angels.

The Spirit of piety and devotion should be the mainspring of life and actions of a Religious. The principal exercises which depend on it, are Meditation, the frequentation of the Sacraments of Confession and Communion, and the Divine Office. Of these we will treat hereafter.

CHAPTER XII.

Religious Modesty.

Let the Sisters ever bear in mind what they are—that is to say, consecrated to God; and in consideration of this quality, let them, according to the Apostle's teaching, "*act as it becometh Saints,*" avoiding all affected gravity in their speech, gestures and countenance, as well as all kinds of familiarity unbecoming in Religious life— such as vulgar expressions and ridiculous actions. On the contrary, their words should be humble and mild, their walk moderate, without running, and their general deportment simple and religious. They should never permit their eyes to wander, especially in the Choir, Refectory, and Chapter-room, or before seculars, whom they should never look fixedly in the face.

The Sisters must avoid all that savors of levity—never striking one another even in play—nor make use of any caress that might excite sensual imaginations, this being strictly forbidden in the Rule.

They should manifest a cordial respect for one another, saluting each other by an inclination of the head when they meet—without, however, stopping to amuse themselves in chatting or conversing, except when necessary, or with permission. They should never scream or speak too loud and with warmth; let them not be precipitate in their conversations, nor interrupt one another, especially when a superior speaks, rather accustoming themselves to yield to one another.

Poverty and religious simplicity must be observed in their dress, which should, however, be always neat and clean, but without affectation or singularity. It is expressly forbidden to make use of any new invention or of a peculiar style of finer or more beautiful cloth, to curl or show their hair, or to be in the least degree over careful or affected in their head-dress. The Mother Superioress must be very careful to retrench everything of the kind, and never allow any Sister to keep what may in the least savor of curiosity, affectation or singularity.

The Sisters should never leave their rooms without being well covered and decently attired. They should never expose their arms, bosom or other parts of the body before any of the Sisters; and in case of sickness this must be done with the greatest possible prudence, delicacy and modesty, being always careful to preserve religious purity.

Let the Mistress of Novices take great care to instruct and exercise them in all the points of Religious Modesty.

INSTRUCTION.

The greatness and sanctity of God, in Whose sight we should continually walk—the presence of Jesus, our Saviour, who according to His promise, is always in the midst of those who are assembled in His name—the Society of the Guardian Angels of the Community, who continually behold the face of God, who see us and always carry their Paradise in our midst—the company of the Sisters who should be revered as Angels on earth—should manifest on the countenance and exterior demeanor of each Sister that respectful reserve, reverence and religious modesty to which the Apostle, St. Paul, exhorts and invites us "*by the gentleness and the modesty of Jesus.*" He refers gentleness to the interior, and modesty to the exterior. As the soul of Jesus was in a continual state of the most profound reverence towards His Divinity, so His exterior deportment and appearance, stamped with grave and perfect modesty, impressed well-disposed souls with a respect of love and of honor. Now, as He should be our model and interior plenitude, we, too, should spread by our exterior the good odor of His grace and spirit.

The Sisters should evince, in all their actions, a Christian and religious modesty, in accordance with the exhortation of the Apostle: *"Let your modesty be known to all men, for the Lord is nigh"* (Philip 4); as though he would say: "He sees you, He is in the midst of you." Let them contemplate and adore Jesus in the most Holy Sacrament as in the centre of their dwelling, and in all places, by the presence of His spirit. But as some of the actions of the Community—for instance, those of the Choir, Chapter and other assemblies, are more serious, they should watch more strictly over themselves and keep their senses mortified from all curiosity. As regards others, namely: entertainments and recreations, which seem to allow more freedom, let them bear in mind these words of St. Paul, as an invariable rule: *"But fornication and all uncleanness, let it not be so much as named among you, as it becometh Saints ; nor obscenity, nor foolish talking, which is to no purpose"* (Ephes. 5)— that is to say, all indecency, and words or actions unbecoming to Religious. St. Paul does not wish us to allude or listen to such things, even though it be only in the narration of past events; and this should be observed to such a degree that if, in the Spiritual Reading at table or in the Community, a Sister should happen to come across a passage descriptive of improper things in the lives of the Saints, or any good author, not even excepting the Sacred Scriptures, the Superioress or the presiding Sister should command it to be omitted, and have read only what follows.

The above words of the Apostle, "*as it becometh Saints,*" show, that as the Sisters are obliged to aspire to a high degree of sanctity, all their words and actions should be holy and worthy of the holiness of their vocation.

CHAPTER XIII.

Mental Prayer.

All the Choir Sisters shall devote the whole of the first hour of the day to Meditation, which is to commence at five o'clock from the Feast of St. Michael until Easter, and at half-past four during the remainder of the year. They will also spend another half hour in the same Exercise every evening at five o'clock, after which they shall recite Matins and Lauds for the following day.

Let all assemble in the Choir or Tribune to make their morning and evening Meditation before the Blessed Sacrament. They should punctually obey the sound of the bell for this Exercise—imagining they hear the words that St. Martha addressed to Mary Magdalen: "*The Lord is there and asks for you.*" They should go with alacrity, and, like this "lover of Jesus," cast themselves at His sacred Feet. No one is allowed to exempt herself without necessity and without the Mother Superioress' permission Those who are employed with the boarders or at other offices must not fail to make their Meditation at the time prescribed for them.

The Lay Sisters shall make only a half hour's Meditation in the morning.

INSTRUCTION.

Prayer, the daily bread of the soul, is not less necessary than bread is for the nourishment of the body. It is the celestial manna which God causes to descend abundantly in the desert of Religion; and each one should gather it every day, like the ancients, according to the measure ordained by God—that is to say, according to her capacity and in proportion to the grace of God. The Sisters should cherish this holy Exercise as the sweetest entertainment and the most delicious banquet of the soul—as the most useful and important employment of their time, and as the principal aid towards the attainment of Religious Perfection. They who can spare a quarter of an hour or more should deem it well employed when spent in solitude with our Lord—reposing at His Feet, and, like St. Mary Magdalen, listening to His interior conversation. We read in the Book of Wisdom: "There is no bitterness in His speech, and His intercourse has no weariness, but rather pleasure and joy." Herein we may easily recognize the true daughters of His family, who hasten to prayer as to a spiritual banquet, relishing therein interior sweetness; whereas mercenaries and slaves, being full of disgust, disquietude and coldness during this holy Exercise, go to it as to a place of trial, because, by their idle discourses, curiosity and dissipation, they seek their consolation in exterior things; in which, however, they will never find the satisfaction they expect. They resemble the Prodigal who, having left his father's house, desired to still his hunger with the food of swine, but even this was refused him.

To guard against errors and illusions, the Sisters shall manifest their interior to the Rev. Mother, or, with her permission, to the Spiritual Father, making known their manner of prayer with simplicity and confidence; giving an account of what they experience therein—of the facility or the difficulty they meet with, and the profit they derive therefrom.

The principal exercise of Meditation is not so much in the understanding by fine thoughts and curious conceptions, but rather in the will by diverse affections, from which should be drawn strong and efficacious resolutions for the correction of faults and the practice of virtue. These resolutions, when solidly grounded and faithfully executed, will form permanent dispositions; and in this consists the most essential fruit of Meditation. Hence, that which is made in the evening may be but the repetition of the morning's Meditation by way of application and particular affections. The Mother Superioress may, however, have other points read if she thinks proper.

At the most convenient time after Meditation, the Sisters should make a brief review of the faults they may have committed, and the principal points and affections that may have moved them during the hour of prayer, in order to select the most striking and that which made the deepest impression, to serve as a subject of frequent elevations of the soul during the day, and as a means of preserving the spirit of prayer and recollection amid the diversity of daily occupations. Thus the Ursulines will become true Daughters of prayer, and accomplish the saying of our Lord: " Pray always, and never desist "— not, indeed, by a continual application, which is impossible in this life, but by the spirit of prayer, by obedience and the practice of virtue.

CHAPTER XIV.

Confession and Holy Communion.

All the Sisters shall go to confession to the ordinary Confessor twice a week — on the eve of Communion, and let no one be permitted to defer it until the morning, except in case of necessity and with the Mother Superioress' permission. When there are two Communions immediately following each other, the Sisters need not go to confession a second time, except in case of a particular necessity—as one Communion is the most excellent preparation for another.

The ordinary Confessor of the House should be well qualified for this office by his prudence, capacity and piety. Having been acknowledged as such by the Superioress, she should ask the Bishop to appoint him and give him his approbation. The same must be done when it will be found expedient to change him.

The Community should also have a Spiritual Father Director, which office may be filled either by the Confessor or by another, to whom the Rt. Rev. Bishop shall give what authority he thinks proper for the spiritual and temporal government of the Monastery, requiring, from time to time, an account of the same. Said Director may be either a resident of the same place or otherwise, provided he be free of access, and that he be present in cases of urgent necessity.

When a young lady enters to become a Religious, she should be exhorted to make a General Confession of her whole life before she receives the Holy Habit; and at the time of her Profession, let her make one from the date of her entrance.

Each Sister should make an annual Confession every year, either during the Retreat or at some other time. She may have an extraordinary Confessor, if such be her desire.

In accordance with the decree of the holy Council of Trent, the Mother Superioress should offer the Community an extraordinary Confessor two or three times a year. He should be a learned person, of well-known zeal and charity, and specially approved by the Bishop to that effect. He may be called in for the Feast of the Presentation, before the Renewal of Vows, or in Advent and Lent. Should any Sister ask for an extraordinary Confessor for the direction of her conscience, the Rev. Mother may grant her request, if she deem it expedient, provided he be approved as mentioned above.

The Sisters shall generally receive Holy Communion twice a week—on Sundays and Thursdays—besides the feasts of obligation. However, when these latter fall on Wednesday or Friday, they will not make the Communion of Thursday. The Mother-Superioress may permit some extraordinary Communions, either to the Community in general or to the Sisters in particular, when circumstances or necessity require it.

The Novices shall receive the Sacraments as their Mistress may judge them capable. She may permit or refuse them more than one Communion a week.

The Lay Sisters shall receive Holy Communion only on Sundays, on the Feasts of our Lord, those of our Blessed Lady, of St. Ursula, our Mother St. Angela, our Father,

St. Augustin, and whenever the Mother Superioress permits them.

All the Choir and Lay Sisters, including the Novices, must assist at the Holy Sacrifice of the Mass every day, unless prevented by some notable hindrance. All should assist with the greatest possible tranquillity and recollection of mind, preparing themselves to communicate spiritually when the Priest receives sacramentally. That this rule may be the more easily observed, more than one Mass should be said in the Convent Chapel.

INSTRUCTION.

On Confession and Communion.

These two Sacraments of our Salvation should be cherished as the most worthy effects of God's Providence in His Church; as the most precious pledges of His love, and as the most efficacious means of recovering and preserving the interior life, or of advancing therein. Hence, all the Sisters should excite in themselves an interior thirst, an ardent desire to receive these Sacraments, endeavoring to approach them with a reverence full of love, and a love full of fear and respect.

There is, however, a marked difference between these two Sacraments; that of Penance is a Sacrament of the dead—that is to say, it has been instituted for sinners who are dead to grace, to enable them to rise from this death of sin to a life of grace; whereas the Sacrament of the Altar is a Sacrament of the living, which it is not permitted to receive in a state of death—or mortal sin. The former gives life; the latter strengthens and preserves in us the life thus received. Jesus, to signify the one and the other, says: "I have come that they may have life"—that is to say, by Penance, "and that they may have it more abundantly"—namely, by Holy Communion.

The Council of Trent ordains that whosoever feels his conscience burdened with mortal sin, shall go to Confession before approaching the Holy Table, bearing in mind these words of St. Paul: "Let man prove himself, and then eat of this bread."

Let us add, that in Confession the soul humbles herself; but in Holy Communion, our Lord exalts her; in the one, she receives the pardon of her sins; in the other, an abundance of grace; in the one, she divests herself of the old Adam, and in the other, she clothes herself with the new—who is Christ Jesus, our Lord.

Although every action of a Religious should be performed in a Christian and religious spirit, these should surpass them all. We shall, therefore, propose some dispositions for the reception of both Sacraments, which the Sisters should endeavor to obtain from God.

CHAPTER XV.

Dispositions Requisite for a Good Confession.

The examination of conscience should be made with great care and diligence before Confession; but as amendment and interior renovation should be the principal fruits of this Sacrament, the Sisters must try to be short in their self-examination, not employing, as a general thing, more time than would be required to say one, or at most two, *Misereres*. Let them, however, carefully exercise themselves in forming acts of humility before the Supreme Majesty of God—at the sight of their own nothingness, their sins and ingratitude—acts of lively and sovereign contrition proceeding from love for their offended God, combined with a zealous desire to avenge on themselves, by worthy fruits of penance, the injury done to God by sin. Finally, they should make a firm resolution to amend and correct themselves. It would be very good, at each Confession, to take to heart some particular fault to combat or eradicate; and in this they will be greatly assisted by the grace of the Sacrament.

The Sisters should accuse themselves in Confession with great humility, contrition and simplicity. Humility will make the true penitent present herself before her Confessor as a criminal deserving condemnation before the tribunal of her Sovereign Judge; nevertheless, she must have great confidence of obtaining from him, as from her Saviour, the pardon of her sins. Simplicity will make her accuse herself of her sins with candor as she knows them, and as clearly and briefly as possible, avoiding all evasions, detailed accounts, excuses, questions, uneasiness of scruples, and a too exact scrutiny of her actions—all of which are only amusements and often an abuse of the Sacrament. The best confessions are those which are made in fewer words, with less research, but with all the more interior sentiment.

The Sisters should especially avoid recalling and confessing the sins of their past life, and rarely even those of the preceding confessions—at least, not without the Confessor's permission.

The soul, life and perfection of the Sacrament of Penance consist in that perfect sorrow for sin which proceeds from the pure love of God, and a determined resolution of never offending Him deliberately. Without this disposition, confession would be as a body without a soul. Let the Sisters endeavor to awaken these sentiments in their hearts during their accusation, but especially at the moment of absolution. Thus, did Magdalen act at the feet of Jesus, not ceasing to wash them with her tears until she heard from Her Master and Confessor the consoling words, "All thy sins are forgiven thee."

After Confession the Sisters should remain collected and offer to God a contrite, humble, and renewed heart, begging Him to supply by His Mercy for the deficiencies of their contrition, and thanking him for the grace received in the Sacrament, saying, with the Psalmist: "My soul bless the Lord, and let all that is within me magnify His holy Name." (Psalm 102.)

The following are six graces and favors received by absolution: (1) God pardons our sins—*propitiatur omnibus iniquitatibus.* (2) He heals the diseases that remain as scars on our souls, enclining us to evil—*Sanat omnes infirmitates.* (3) He redeems and delivers our soul from eternal death—*Redimet de interitu animam nostram.* (4) He crowns us in His Mercy and pours His graces into our souls—*Coronat in misericordia miserationibus.* (5) He enables us to accomplish our good desires—*Replet in bonis desiderium.* (6) We are changed and renewed by His grace, and receive, as it were, a spiritual youth to commence serving God with new fervor—*Renovabit ut aquila juventus.* It is always good to perform the penance imposed as soon as possible, and with the dispositions just indicated.

CHAPTER XVI.

Dispositions for Holy Communion.

Let the Sisters from every part of their Monastery turn their heart to Jesus in this divine Sacrament as to the "Tree of Life," beautiful to the sight and delicious to the taste, planted in the midst of their earthly paradise. Here is the centre and the love of their hearts, to whom all should be referred—the soul of the mystical body of their Community, from which they are to derive spirit, life and energy. Hence, they should labor, converse, and keep themselves in the presence of Jesus and of His sacred Humanity, which dwells in the Tabernacle of their Church; they should form His spiritual court and there adore their Lord and Spouse, cultivating a particular love for these visits. If they have any sentiment of devotion it should be manifested towards this precious pledge and sacred furnace of divine love—which sends forth its flames from the Altar into our hearts to attract and unite them to itself.

In order to derive from Holy Communion all the profit that God intended, the Sisters should not only have purified their conscience in confession from the stain of mortal sin, which, by the mercy of God, should never find access into the Monastery; but also, inasmuch as possible, from the lighter venial faults. They should always be actuated by dispositions of sincere devotion, being careful never to approach the Holy Table through habit or routine, but each time excite in their souls the same fervor as if it were the first and last Communion of their life.

In ancient times God caused the Manna to fall in the desert, but first sent a fresh dew to prepare the banquet, and then caused the ardent rays of the sun to dissolve it. In like manner, we may distinguish three things in Holy Communion, namely, the preparation before communicating, the act of receiving and the thanksgiving. We shall, therefore, suggest some dispositions for each, which the Sisters may cultivate, or other similar sentiments with which our dear Lord may inspire them.

Before Holy Communion they should excite in themselves an ardent longing for this heavenly Bread, sighing for the hour and the moment when they will have the happiness of receiving it, exclaiming, with the Psalmist: "When shall I appear before the face of my God? O, God of Power, how lovely are Thy Tabernacles! My soul is consumed with the desire of approaching Thee!" It is of great importance to correct the pusillanimity of those who through servile fear and scruples go to Holy Communion, as it were, by force, ever considering themselves unworthy. On the one hand, we should humble ourselves profoundly, and say thrice, with the Centurion, "Lord, I am not worthy that Thou shouldst enter under my roof;" the first time, at the sight and in acknowledgment of our nothingness; the second time, because of our sins and ingratitude; and the third time, in adoration of the Supreme Majesty and holiness of Jesus, whom we are about to receive. Penetrated with awe, we may exclaim, with the humble St. Francis: "Lord who art Thou, and who am I?" But, on the other hand, let us arouse ourselves and listen to the sacred words addressed to the heart of the Beloved: "Descend quickly, for this day I must abide with you;" and, like Zaccheus, let us welcome Him joyously into the dwelling of our souls. The triple preparation before communion consist, therefore: (1) in a spiritual hunger or fervent desire of communicating; (2) in the three kinds of humiliation proposed above; and, lastly, in that love and confidence with which Jesus comes to us, and with which we should approach Him.

While communicating we should humble ourselves, and say with St. Elizabeth: "Whence is it that the Mother of my Saviour, namely, the Holy Eucharist—nay, my Lord Himself, comes to me!" or, with St. Peter, "Depart from me Lord, for I am a sinful creature." But, then, let us raise our confidence and rejoice with the infant St. John in the presence of Jesus, saying: "Come quickly, Lord, and do not delay." To these practices of devotion we should add an entire and unreserved donation and oblation of ourselves to Him who gives Himself entirely to us in this Mystery; offering our Hearts to His Heart, our minds to His—in a word, giving all for all.

After communion we should carefully recollect ourselves and enter into the oratory of our hearts, there to remain in solitude with our beloved Spouse. Let us receive from Him the thoughts and sentiments with which He will inspire us; for this end we should try sometimes to be satisfied with being interiorly in His presence, and be very attentive to all that He may say to us; and if He permits us to think, or to tell Him anything, let us lay open to Him the wounds of our soul, as to our physician, and all the secrets of our heart, as to our dearest Friend. Let us make a thousand protestations of our desire to love and serve Him; let us beg Him for all the graces and favors of which He knows we stand in need, and ask particularly for some new blessing, and then repeat the verse: "*Bless the Lord, O, my soul,*" etc., in thanksgiving for the six graces and favors mentioned in the preceding Chapter, and which we receive most abundantly in Holy Communion.

Finally, let us not fail while in the presence of Jesus and possessing Him in our souls to make the following reflections: Ah! what cannot so powerful, so truly present, and so active a God do in a soul that is well prepared to receive the impressions of divine grace! For He is within us, with all the power of His divine Love, to perform great things in our behalf; and we may not doubt a single Communion might suffice for a lifetime and produce fruits for an endless eternity.

Glory to Jesus! I give myself to Thee that Thou mayest act in me according to the plenitude of Thy holy designs. Destroy and annihilate in me all the obstacles to Thy grace and render me worthy to serve and love Thee now and in Eternity.

CHAPTER XVII.

The Divine Office.

The Sisters shall say no other office than that of the Blessed Virgin, which all are to say together in the Choir, slowly, distinctly and intelligibly—modulating the voice in the middle of each verse—making a pause between the verses, and carefully observing the punctuation and the accent. This should be done with all the more exactness, as the Scriptures declare: *"Cursed is he who doth the work of God negligently."* The Sisters should, therefore, endeavor to bring two dispositions to this holy Exercise, viz: devotion, by interior recollection, and respect, by exterior Modesty, remembering these words of the Rule: "Let no one do anything in the Oratory but that for which it is destined;" and these of our Lord, "My House is a house of prayer."

On Sundays and festivals of obligation the Sisters shall sing or say the Vespers of the day, according to the Breviary. The Grand Office is to be said on Christmas and the three days of Tenebræ; on the feast of All Saints they shall say Vespers, Matins, with the nine Lessons and Lauds of the Dead, for All Souls' Day, besides the office of the Blessed Virgin, which is not interrupted on that day.

This same Office is to be said at the decease of a Sister of the House.

The Lay Sisters shall daily say ten *Paters*

and *Ave Marias* for Matins and Lauds; five for Prime, Tierce, Sexte, and None; and three for Vespers and Complin. When the Grand Office is said they will say thirty-three *Paters* and *Aves*, besides the Beads, which all must say every day.

Let no one absent herself from Divine Office except in case of sickness, or when occupied with the Boarders, or at other duties which cannot be deferred to another time. In other cases of real necessity the Mother Superioress is to judge, according to God, if a dispensation be required.

It is never permitted to speak, laugh, read letters, or do anything else in the Choir during Divine Office, at which time the Sisters should have no book except the Breviary or Office Book. They should behave in the Choir with great modesty, recollection and becoming gravity—never looking about, but maintaining a uniform posture whether standing or sitting, inclined or kneeling, as it is prescribed in the Ceremonial. The Directress of the Choir should see that this rule is observed, and notify those who fail. Let her be very careful in having the particular ceremonies rehearsed whenever the Mother Superioress deems it expedient.

Those who come late to the Choir, the Office being already commenced, should prostrate themselves, and then remain on their knees until the end of the Psalm, when they may rise and repair to their places. The Sisters should never leave the Choir before the end of the Divine Office, except in case of urgent necessity and with the permission of the Superioress or the presiding Sister.

Matins and Lauds are to be said at half-past five in the evening; Prime, Tierce, Sexte and None immediately after the Morning Meditation.

The first Mass, called the "Conventual Mass," is to be said at six o'clock in Summer and at half-past six in Winter. All must assist, and on appointed days receive Holy Communion at this Mass, no one being permitted to defer it to the second Mass, except with the Rev. Mother's permission. The second Mass is generally said about nine o'clock.

Vespers and Complin are to be said on week days at three o'clock; on Sundays and

Festivals at half-past two, and when there is a sermon at two o'clock. During Lent, Vespers should be said on week days at half-past ten, and Complin at a quarter to five, except when there is a sermon, in which case it may be said afterwards.

INSTRUCTION.

The Militant Church on earth is a living image of the Triumphant Church in Heaven. Now, as the Angels and the Blessed are constantly praising God, so it is one of the noblest and most important duties of souls consecrated to God in the Religious Life to sing the divine praises. It is but just that they should commence in life the holy Exercise which they are destined to continue throughout eternity, and that being assembled in the Choir they should, in the name of the whole Church, render public glory to God, who is either entirely unknown and blasphemed or served with indifference in the greater part of the habitable world.

In assisting at the Divine Office the Sisters should strive to unite themselves (1) to the celestial canticles of the Angels and to their sentiments of fear and awe before the Majesty of God. (2) To the interior exultations of the most blessed Virgin before her little Jesus in His Infancy, and (3) to the sublime adoration of the deified soul of Jesus from the first moment of His Incarnation.

These reflections should occupy, inspire and ravish them during the celebration of the divine praises.

CHAPTER XVIII.

The Prayers and Good Works to be Offered for the Souls of the Deceased Sisters, Founders, and Benefactors of the House.

When it shall please God to call to Himself a member of the Community—whether a Choir or Lay Sister, or even a Novice—besides what is prescribed in the Ceremonial for the funeral rites, let the holy Mass be offered for her during thirty days and the *De Profundis* be said in the Refectory after meals during the same space of time. The portion of the deceased should during this interval be daily given to a poor person, who shall be requested to pray for her. Let each Sister say in private three Nocturns of three Lessons, and make five Communions for her. The Lay Sisters shall say thirty-three *Paters* and *Ave Marias* for the Grand Office and fifteen for the Nocturns of Three Lessons. The Community is exhorted to offer all the prayers, Communions, penances, and other good works during these thirty days for the repose of the deceased; and, as has already been mentioned, the discipline shall be taken once in common for the same intention.

The same is to be done for the Archbishop or Bishop, the Director and Confessor who die in the exercise of their charge. The Mother Superioress, with her Council, may order something more in proportion to the length and value of their services. She shall also prescribe the prayers that are to be said for those to whom the Monastery is under special obligations.

When it has pleased God to call a Sister to Himself it should be made known to the other Houses of the Congregation as soon as possible, that they may say the prayers prescribed—namely, have three Masses and a General Communion offered for the deceased, and say the Vespers, a Nocturn of three Lessons and Lauds of the Dead. The Superioress may, however, by the advice of her Council, order something more if the deceased has been a Superior or an elderly Sister who has long served the Order.

For the fathers and mothers of the Religious, as also for their brothers and sisters deceased above the age of twelve, a Mass is to be offered, and each sister shall say in private one Nocturn of three Lessons for the Dead. In order that our Communities may prove their gratitude towards their Founders and Benefactors, the *De Profundis* shall be said every evening after the Examination of Conscience for the deceased Sisters and Benefactors, adding a special prayer for the person who founded or endowed the Monastery. Besides the *De Profundis* and other prayers which should be said for him or her during an entire year, a Mass shall be perpetually offered for him or her on the anniversary of his or her death, together with the Vespers, a Nocturn of three Lessons and Lauds for the Dead. The Superioress, with her Council, shall ordain with charity for other benefactors.

A Mass and the same Office is to be said four times a year on the first favorable occasion after the solemn feasts of Easter, Pentecost, All Saints and Christmas—not only for the deceased Religious of our own Congregation, but for all deceased Ursulines and for the souls of the Founders, Benefactors, Confessors, Directors, Fathers and Mothers of the Religious in the Monastery.

INSTRUCTION.

The Communion of Saints unites us not only with the living, but also with the Blessed who enjoy the vision of God and who assist us by their prayers, and with the Faithful departed who are in Purgatory, and whom we should relieve by our prayers and good works; for we all form but one body, of which Jesus Christ is the Head. We should, therefore, practise the same charity towards the departed souls, as we would wish them to exercise in our behalf when they will be before God. Hence, the Sisters should be very fervent and exact in acquitting themselves of the prayers and other sacred duties which are prescribed in behalf of their deceased Sisters and the other Benefactors of this Institute.

Death should be considered by true Christians not only as a common debt of Nature, or as the punishment of sin, but also as an effect of the death of the Son of God, of which we have received a character in Baptism, giving us a resemblance to Jesus dying—a resemblance which could not be perfected except by our own death. Moreover, as Religious Life is but a school in which we are to learn to die well, the Sisters should early accustom themselves not to fear this supreme passage, and to be always resigned to the will of God in life as well as in death. They should even desire this last hour in order to be freed from sin, from the world and all terrestrial objects, from their flesh and themselves, to become conformable to Jesus dying and to be united with Him forever. These are the effects which the love of God and the thought of death produce in holy souls, and which we ought to consider in the Sisters whom God calls to Himself.

PART II.

Treating of the Exterior Regulations and Observances of the Monastery.

CHAPTER I.

On Cloister, the Entrance and the Parlors.

The decree of the holy Council of Trent relative to the Cloister shall be inviolably observed. We here give it in the exact words: "Let it not be lawful for any Re-"ligious to leave her Monastery after her "Profession, not even for a time, however "short it may be, nor under any pretext "whatsoever, unless it be for a legitimate "cause approved by the Bishop. As to en- "tering the enclosure of the Monastery, let "it not be permitted to any one—whatever "may be their age, standing, or sex—with- "out an express and written permission "from the Bishop, under the penalty of ex- "communication incurred by the act itself." This permission should be given only in cases of necessity, and can be granted only by the Bishop or by the one whom his Lordship authorizes to act in his name. We must, however, except cases for which the Holy See itself has granted some permissions, as also those of necessity, namely, exceptions by right of office or duty, as the Confessor, the physician, the surgeon and the laborers. Boarders, also, are permitted to enter, to be instructed according to the end of the Institute.

There are four canonical cases in which the Religious are permitted to leave their Monastery, namely, pestilence, war, fire and famine. These cases excepted, should any necessity arise, to call a Sister from one morastery to another, she must first obtain her letter of Obedience from the Rt. Rev. Bishop, or from him who holds his place.

When any one enters the enclosure through necessity or with permission, let two sisters accompany him where his duty calls, and the bells be rung that the Religious may be on their guard and retire into their cells or office rooms, so as not to be met on the way. The same is to be done when the person leaves. Those who come in should remain no longer than is necessary to do the work required.

The Confessor, while hearing a sick Sister's confession, should always be seen by the two sisters who will have accompanied him to the room, the door of which must be left partly open.

The Priest or Confessor may enter for the administration of the Sacraments of Penance, Holy Communion and Extreme Unction, as, also, to console the sick in their last moments, and for the funeral rites —besides other cases of necessity, decided by the Mother Superioress. It would be advisable for him to wear the surplice on these occasions—and that the Sister

Portress, accompanied by her assistant or the Infirmarian, should conduct him to the Infirmary, following and keeping sight of him wherever he may go.

The principal door of the enclosure, and the small one set in the large, if there be any such, should have two different locks; the key of one is to be kept by the Superioress and that of the other by the principal Portress.

When it shall be necessary to open the door and the Rev. Mother is unable to go, she may give her key to any one she thinks proper, not, however, to the Portress.

These doors should never be left ajar, but be closed immediately; hence, no one should remain there to speak. Nothing should be taken in through the doors when it can be passed through the Turn—and they must not be opened without necessity and the Mother Superioress' permission.

From Easter to St. Michael's, the doors and Turns may be opened at 4:30, A. M., and closed at 8 P. M., but from St. Michael's to Easter they should not be opened before 6 A. M., and closed at 6:30, P. M., unless some urgent necessity oblige otherwise, in which case the Mother Superioress may permit it.

Neither the Sisters nor others in the house should go to the parlor without the permission of the Superioress, nor without a companion whom the Rev. Mother is to appoint, and who should place herself where she can always see the parties and hear their conversation—except when matters of conscience or other important affairs are discussed, with the Mother Superioress' consent.

The Holy Council of Trent recommends that there be as few entrances (or doors) as possible to Monasteries for women. Hence besides the Confessional, there should not be more than five gratings without the express and written permission of the Bishop. (1) That of the Church, in the centre of which should be a small door, that is to be opened for the reception of Holy Communion, blessed ashes, palms and candles, and whenever the Superioress may judge proper. At the Vesture and Profession of Novices a part of the grating may be opened. The second grating shall be for the transaction of business, on the inside and outside of which should be a small table that may serve for writing, signing documents, counting money, and other similar purposes. In this grating there should be a door through which documents, lawyer's papers, etc., may be passed. The key is to be kept by the Superioress. Besides these there may be two gratings for the Boarders' Reception rooms, and a fifth for that of the Sisters.

The Religious should never stop to speak in the parlor without lowering the veil to cover their face—except with the Rev. Mother's permission, when speaking to their near relatives or to persons of a certain position with whom they may raise their veil, but then let them keep their eyes modestly cast down.

The Portress must, each evening, leave the keys of the parlors and Turns with the Superioress, and return for them in the morning.

The Sisters should endeavor, as a general rule, not to remain longer than a half hour with seculars in the parlor, and never to go during the hours of Meditation and Divine Office, except it be for urgent and important business, and with the Mother Superioress' sanction.

They should always be careful to edify their visitors, never speaking of vanities, curiosities or worldly news. They must also avoid repeating indiscriminately to the other Sisters what they may have heard — remembering that they " *should be crucified to the world, and the world to them*"—that they have no longer anything to do with its pomps and vanities, which they have renounced in Baptism, and by their Religious Profession. Finally, they should fear to lose, during a quarter of an hour spent in the parlor, that treasure of peace and interior recollection, the acquisition of which may have cost them much time and labor.

INSTRUCTION.

Exterior Solitude consists principally in the Monastic Enclosure, which is, as it were, a barrier of separation between the world and the cloister—for a true Religious should be dead to the world, and live only for Jesus; according to these beautiful words of St. Paul, "*you are dead, and your life is hidden in God with Christ Jesus our Lord.*"

The holy and ineffable solitude of Jesus during the nine months He reposed in Mary's virginal womb; His solitude with Mary during His sacred infancy; His forty days' retirement in the desert; the many nights He spent in the mountains; and lastly, His loneliness on the Cross, should serve as so many powerful motives to draw souls into solitude with Him, as so many objects of veneration and examples for imitation; finally, as living fountains to vivify the spirit of retirement and interior solitude, and to shower upon us graces from their plenitude.

CHAPTER II.

The Refectory, the Repast, and Recreation.

The Sisters shall eat together in the Refectory, and they are not permitted to eat elsewhere, except in case of sickness, in the Infirmary, or in the cell, if the sister is not able to go to the Infirmary. If the Mother Superioress deems it necessary for a convalescent Sister, she may allow her to eat in the open air.

The treatment in the Refectory should be as uniform as possible, and the Sister Dispenser shall not be permitted to gratify any one. Nevertheless, great consideration should be paid to the necessities of the infirm, the convalescent, and in general, to the wants of all the Sisters, according to that charity so strongly recommended in the Rule of our Father, St. Augustin, and as the Superioress, or under her, the Sister Housekeeper, may ordain. Theirs alone is the duty to see that the Community, as well as the infirm, be treated with sufficiency and cleanliness—always, however, in accordance with Religious Poverty and Simplicity. When there is any cause for complaint they alone should give the required admonition and see that the fault is repaired. It is very expressly forbidden to complain or to speak of the food and drink: the Sisters should rather accustom themselves to suffer privations in their necessities as an effect of Holy Poverty.

The Mother Superioress, or in her absence the Mother Assistant or the eldest Sister, shall say the *Benedicite* according to the Roman Breviary.

Let each of the Choir Sisters read and serve at table in her turn, as shall be marked on a catalogue placed at the door of the Refectory. The Mother Superioress is exempted from these practices, as are also those whom she thinks proper to dispense for just reasons.

The Spiritual Reading, which is the food of the soul, shall be continued during the whole time of the first table, at dinner and supper.

At dinner, on Fridays, fast days, and during the whole of Lent, the Reader shall begin by a chapter of the Constitutions. On the first Friday of each month the entire Directory is to be read—without anything else. Should this day be a feast and the preceding one a fast day, it should be read on the latter day, or on the following Saturday. At the evening meal, on days of abstinence, they shall read only the Martyrology and a chapter of the Constitutions. On fast days there will be no

Spiritual Reading at the evening meal.

After dinner and supper the Sisters shall have an hour for recreation, during which they may converse among themselves religiously and with edification, but also with gayety and becoming freedom; avoiding, however, all vulgarity, harshness and contestation in their conversations. Let the presiding Sister pay special attention to these points. She may suggest witty and recreative doubts to some, but let them be such as require no serious application of the mind—and this only when she thinks proper, as it is not obligatory. Those who wish may do some light work during this time, but without too much eagerness.

The Sisters should play no game but what is proper, and sanctioned by the Superioress, who may permit same in the Infirmary for the diversion of the sick and convalescent. Pet animals, such as little dogs, squirrels, birds, etc., should not be tolerated in the Monastery.

Instead of recreation on Friday evening, let Chapter be held at half-past seven. The Sisters shall also abstain from recreation on the evening of vigils of great feasts, viz: that of Pentecost, Assumption, Our Father, St. Augustin, and All Saints, on the three days of Tenebræ, there will be neither noon nor evening recreation, to honor the silence of Jesus during His dolorous Passion; the same is to be observed on days when the Blessed Sacrament is exposed. The Sisters are, however, permitted on these days to walk alone in the garden or elsewhere.

INSTRUCTION.

The Sisters should bear in mind these words of St. Paul: " Whether you eat or drink, or do anything else, whatsoever, do all for the glory of God." Now, as sensuality may very easily glide into our eating and drinking, under pretext of necessity, it is very important to glorify God in this corporal refreshment by always practising some mortification at our meals, and, like St. Bernard, who went to table as to the torture, the Sisters should consider it a great penance and humiliation to be thus subjected to the requirements of the body.

The spirit of sadness and melancholy consumes interior strength and vigor, and is prejudicial to true devotion, whereas the joy of the Holy Ghost communicates to the heart an interior happiness which manifests itself in the exterior during the religious recreations, and in the prompt and cheerful discharge of all the duties of our state. It is the proof of a quiet mind, a peaceful conscience, and a submissive will. Peace of soul, and the spirit of liberty of the children of God, nourish and support, fervor, and enable us to bear the yoke of Jesus with ease and unction, and to find Hif burden light. Hence, all the Sisters are exhorted by the Apostle to preserve a constant cheerfulness and contentment in God. *"Rejoice in the Lord; I say once more, rejoice."* But, that this joy may be moderate, and that it may not betray itself in loud laughter, and other unbecoming acts and gestures, he adds; *"Let your modesty be known to all men, for the Lord is nigh."*

CHAPTER III.

The Dormitory, the Cells, and Repose.

Each of the Sisters, except the sick and those actually employed in their service, should, if possible, have a bedroom to herself.

The dormitory, which should be made to lock, shall be closed about nine o'clock in the evening, and the keys are to be taken to the Mother Superior's room. The Sisters should walk about silently in the cells and dormitory, making as little noise as possible.

Let no one be permitted to keep anything locked, except what belongs to her office or employment. The Superioress must have free access to everything she deems necessary; she should visit the different offices and the Sisters' rooms from time to time. This should be done at least once a month, or whenever she thinks proper — to the end that no singularity may glide into the Monastery. Every evening, after night prayer, the Sister appointed to make the visit of the rooms, should see that all are in bed and that their lights are extinguished. This is done, not only for the sake of order, but also to guard against accidents by fire.

A lighted lamp may be kept all night at one end of the dormitory, as a precaution in case of accidents. The Mother Superioress should charge one of the Sisters to light and extinguish it at an appointed hour, as also to close all the doors and windows.

The Sisters are not permitted to enter one another's cells or office-rooms without permission, except it be to say only a few words. They should never take or read anything in the rooms without permission, this being allowed only to the Superioress, in all places and at all times.

When two or more are together in one room, it should not be locked from the inner side.

The furniture of the cells should be simple, modest, and convenient. The bed is to be of medium size, with four posts, to hold the mosquito-bar, which may be of white linen or cotton, but without fringe or ornament of any kind. The bed should be furnished with a straw-bed, mattress, and bolster, but no pillow (except for the sick), and with linen sheets and two coverlets. No other singular or superfluous article should be permitted.

The Sisters are not allowed to select their cells; the Superioress, or by her order, the Assistant, shall assign a room to each one.

The Mother Superioress may, at times, require the Sisters to change their cells, either to exercise them in the virtue of detachment, or for other reasons. They should not, as a general rule, occupy the same room more than three years, and when they change, they should take all the furniture except the wardrobe; but even this is left to the prudence of the Superioress.

INSTRUCTION.

It was very humiliating to the Eternal Son of God, to condescend, in assuming our flesh, to subject Himself to the necessity of sleep, which suspends the use of reason, and renders us similar to the brute. Now, as Jesus wished to sanctify our repose by His, we should honor His by ours. Hence, the Sisters should endeavor, each night, to unite their sleep to the eternal repose of our divine Lord in the bosom of God His Father, or to the repose of the Child Jesus on His dear Mother's breast, or in the crib; or, again, to the sleep of Jesus in the ship, or to the last sleep of death to which He subjected Himself on the Cross and in the Sepulchre. They should also honor Jesus spending the night in prayer, and the Angels and Blessed in Heaven, who sing the praises of God without intermission, day and night— beseeching them to love Him for them while they sleep, to satisfy the demands of nature.

The cell should serve each Sister as a place of retirement and solitude with our divine Lord. She should listen to her good Angel, saying to her, as to the holy father, St. Arsenius: "*Be seated, read, and pray.*" Like the saintly Thomas à Kempis, she should find her peace and tranquillity only in her cell, her book, and her Crucifix. Let her, therefore, frequently withdraw into the solitude of her room, and, seated on the kneeling bench of her Oratory, with a pious book in her hand, place herself in spirit at the feet of Jesus, and like the dear lover, St. Mary Magdalene, listen attentively to His divine words.

CHAPTER IV.

The Infirmary and the Care of the Sick.

If the convenience of the House permit it, the Infirmary should be separated from the Dormitories and other regular places, not only to be out of reach of the noise of those who pass to and fro, but also for several other reasons. There should be several rooms, if possible, and two or more beds in each. The apartments should be well ventilated, and so situated that they may have the benefit of the best air, but supplied with good windows and shutters. Where this is customary, the Infirmaries may be matted, but not carpeted, unless it be a piece of carpet at the doors or other crevices through which the draught might penetrate. There must be a fire in these rooms, when necessary. The beds should be of a larger size than those in common use, and are to be furnished with feather-beds, good mattresses, bolsters and pillows, as necessity may require; also with cotton or linen mosquito-bars, but without fringe or trimmings; these may be made of netting in summer.

As soon as a Sister feels ill—of a fever or any other notable indisposition — she should inform the Superioress, who shall have her removed to the Infirmary without delay; charitably providing for all her necessities—and this, without exception of persons, for all are the servants of Jesus Christ, daughters of the same Monastery and Sisters in our Lord. The Rev. Mother should frequently visit and console the sick, send for the physician when necessary, and be careful not to leave them in want of anything, seeing that what has been ordered is faithfully performed by those in charge, who shall frequently give her an account of the same. Should the fever continue, the patient ought to go to Confession on the fifth day, at the latest, and if the illness increases, she should receive the last Sacraments while in a state of consciousness. Even Extreme Unction should not be deferred to the last extremity. The sick should be frequently visited by the Superioress or those appointed by her, and even by the Director or Confessor of the Community.

As long as the sick remain in the Infirmary, they are under the charge of the principal Infirmarian, whom they must obey in all that concerns the treatment of their complaint, their diet and remedies—always endeavoring not to render themselves disagreeable to those who serve them. On the other hand, the Infirmarians should never be rude or negligent— neither should they be excessively delicate in providing for the wants of their patients, being content with what is given them for the sick. The Mother Superioress should often see to this point.

INSTRUCTION.

Our Lord is, according to His word, in the midst of those who are assembled in His name; and He replenishes and sanctifies the communities that are consecrated to His service. The Sisters should, therefore, endeavor to seek and to find Him in all the functions and offices of their Monastery—yet by different means and dispositions: In the Choir, by the spirit of prayer; in the Chapter-room, by humiliation and penance; in the Refectory, by modesty and temperance; in their respective offices, by obedience; in their cells, by recollection; and in their recreations, by joy and liberty of spirit. But in the Infirmary, God is to be found and glorified by the patience of the sufferer, and by the charity of those who attend to her wants. This recalls the beautiful words of St. Paul: *" May the Lord guide your hearts in the Charity of God, and in the patience of Christ Jesus."* Religious life should be a continual exercise of these two virtues and dispositions, as an homage to that Charity of God which is Himself, and to the patience which our Saviour Jesus practised during the whole course of his mortal life.

We have a strong motive to be charitable to the sick, when we remember that our Lord considers as done to Himself, whatever we do for the poor, the infirm, and the needy. Hence, our charity in this respect, should be without measure or limit; and if the Ursulines are to have any peculiar characteristic or preëminence, it should be in this virtue.

Therefore, with due regard for poverty, let them endeavor to provide for the sick in all their necessities—whether of nourishment or remedies—being ready, day and night, to render them service and assistance, and to offer them all the corporal and spiritual relief in their power.

The sick, on the other hand, must practise patience, bearing their sufferings and inconvenience with resignation, meekness and humility. Let them obey the Sister Infirmarian and the physician without murmuring, discontent or inordinate complaints—receiving with good grace and with gratitude, as poor beggars, whatever is done and given them through charity and as an alms. It is, therefore, advisable to take in a good supply of these virtues during health.

Lastly, as our Lord desired to glorify His Father in actions and in suffering, He wishes that we, too, should embrace these two means of sanctification, which are to be found especially in the Infirmary; for here some are called to honor His actions by serving the sick, while others honor His sufferings by their illness; hence, whether we live or die, it should always be for our Lord, as the Apostle teaches.

CHAPTER V.

Of Manual Labor and Spiritual Conferences.

To banish idleness, which is the mother of all evil, there shall be some hours appointed for common work. These may conveniently be from ten to eleven in the morning, and from four to five o'clock in the evening. During these hours the Sisters, who are not occupied in the classes, with the boarders, or in other offices, shall assemble together, and each one should work diligently and faithfully, but without over-eagerness, at some work assigned her by the Rev. Mother, who should always endeavor to be present. In her absence, the Assistant, or another Sister, should be appointed to preside.

In order not to stifle the spirit of piety and devotion, by over-application and attention to manual labor, there should be some Spiritual Reading for about half an hour, or as long as the one who presides may think proper; after which the Sisters may converse among themselves on holy and edifying subjects—the presiding Sister being careful to see that nothing improper is introduced. If the Sisters prefer, they may ask permission to sing some pious canticles. During the evening assembly, the Spiritual Reading should not begin until half-past four. All the Sisters should give special attention to these exercises, as it is one of the principal occupations of the day. For this reason they must avoid all work that demands too great an application of the mind, in order to be perfectly free to give their undivided attention to what is read and to converse on the subject.

The Mother Superioress should see that the Sisters be always provided with some work—not only during these assemblies, but also when not in the Community or occupied in their offices. Work may be taken in from the city, and the Rev. Mother should charge one of the Sisters to receive it—no one else being permitted to accept any such work, even from their near relatives. The Sisters should never inquire for whom the work is destined, nor should seculars be informed by whom it has been done. The Sisters should accept work for the Church in preference to any other, and let them never make anything for show or vanity. When the article is returned to the owner, the price of the same should be received in charity and put in the common treasury. If the House can dispense with it, this income should be devoted to the decoration of the Church.

The Mother Superioress may, in case of necessity, dispense those she thinks proper from assisting at the common work.

INSTRUCTION.

St. Martha's house served our Lord Jesus as a dwelling and place of retreat during the course of His last years on earth. In this abode we find two good sisters: the one serving her Master, the other listening to Him; the one engrossed in attending to His wants, the other seated at His feet, hearkening to His sacred words. Both are very pleasing to God—but the one, in active employment—the other, in the quietude of contemplation. Here, then, is the type and model of Ursuline Monasteries which should serve, not as a transient asylum, but as a permanent abode for their Sovereign Lord and Spouse—so that He may be pleased to say: *"This is my habitation for all eternity; here will I dwell, for I have chosen it."* However, let the Sisters unite Martha and Mary—labor and repose, action and prayer. This should be the object of their whole life, not only by alternation—that is, rest following labor, or else, some remaining quiet, while others are at work; but all should, as much as possible, preserve repose in labor, the spirit of prayer in active employments, and interior retreat in exterior conversations — occupying themselves in the functions of the active life only through motives and principles of the contemplative. For this end, work and the Spiritual Reading or Conferences should always be combined.

The Sisters should rejoice in God— through a spirit of devotion, when by their work they gain something for the Church; or through a spirit of poverty, when it serves for the support of the Community— honoring even in this, the Son of God, who is the model of all virtues, and who chose during His entire youth, to work with His own hands at the humble trade of a carpenter, so as to bear the curse of the old Adam— earning His bread by the sweat of His brow.

CHAPTER VI.

The Chapter and Fraternal Correction.

Chapter shall be held at half-past seven P. M. every Friday, except when this day is a feast, when the Blessed Sacrament is exposed, and within the octaves of Easter, Pentecost, the Assumption and the Nativity of the Blessed Virgin; on the Feasts of our Father St. Augustin, our Patroness, St. Ursula, our Blessed Lady's Presentation, All Saints and Christmas. If the Mother Superioress thinks proper, she may hold Chapter on the eves of the above-mentioned festivals. There shall be no Chapter on

Good Friday, but some of the Sisters may, through devotion, make their accusation in the Refectory. The temporal affairs of the House should not be discussed at these Chapters, but at other assemblies convened for that purpose. All the Sisters—whether professed members of the Community, Novices, or Lay Sisters—shall assist at the Chapter, unless prevented by sickness or other legitimate causes.

When the Community is large, one-third, and when less numerous, one-half, of the Sisters should make their accusation at every Chapter. These accusations must include only the ordinary and exterior faults against the Rules and Constitutions, or such others as may draw confusion on the accuser. The Mother Superioress should, however, be careful not to allow anything ridiculous, or calculated to scandalize the other Sisters. If any notable fault has been committed which is known to the whole Community, it may be confessed publicly. The accusations begin by those of the Lay Sisters, who retire and are followed by those of the Novices, who likewise withdraw; these are succeeded by those of the professed members of the Community.

It is not permitted to repeat, out of Chapter, whether that of the correction of faults or that of business transactions, what has been said or done therein, unless it be something edifying that concerns no particular individual. The Sisters should never complain or find fault with the correction or penance imposed. This should always be proportional to the fault. Nevertheless, let it be mild, religious and humiliating, rather than afflicting.

There are three kinds of faults: (1) The slight—such as to come a little late to the observance of the Community, provided this be not habitual or through contempt of the Rule; to make a mistake in reading or in psalmodying; to fall asleep during Divine Office; to laugh immoderately, break silence, or narrate incidents of a wordly nature; to break or spoil anything in the Monastery, and other similar defects which may be committed through inadvertence.

The penance ordinarily imposed for such faults should be a *Pater* and *Ave*, some psalms, holding the arms extended in the form of a cross, prostration, kissing the floor, or others, according to the direction of the Superioress.

(2) There are serious faults committed deliberately or through negligence; for instance, quarreling with one another; using bitter or injurious expressions; reproaching a Sister with a fault which she has repaired; revealing the privacy of Chapter; habitual talking during a considerable time of the hours of silence; obstinacy in excusing oneself; causing disunion among the Sisters by tale-bearing or otherwise; complaints or murmurs against the Superioress; keeping delicacies without necessity or permission; eating in secret, and other similar transgressions.

The penance for faults of this nature should be—to eat on the floor in the middle of the Refectory; to take the discipline; to remain kneeling or prostrate during the repast; to kiss the Sisters' feet; or, to kneel at the door of the Refectory as the Sisters enter or leave, and ask their prayers.

Finally, there are what may be called very grievous faults—for instance, to strike or insult a Sister; to transgress the essence of the vows: for example, to hide or appropriate something of value; to hold familiar, suspicious, and dangerous communications with secular or religious men; writing or receiving letters from them in secret; all that would be a mortal sin against purity; notable contempt of the Rules, Constitutions and Superiors—treating them irreverently or injuriously; drawing others into similar contempt, plots, etc., which, to be classed among the very grievous faults, must be of the nature of a mortal sin.

The penances imposed for such as these should be—disciplines, fasts on bread and water, separation from the Community and confinement to a special apartment for a limited period; deprivation of an active or passive voice in Chapter, for one, two, or three years; to be declared unfit for any charge or office; to lose permanently, or for a specified period, the rank of Profession, and others similar. These penances must never be imposed except when the sin is known, proved, and confessed by the offender. God grant that such penances may never be required as punishments, and if ever used, may it be only as practices of mortification, embraced through devotion.

The Superioress should show herself mild and indulgent toward those who acknowledge their faults; but very firm and severe toward such as are arrogant, presumptuous, harsh, malicious, and obstinate—never pardoning them until they have humbled themselves.

There are three methods of fraternal correction, indicated by our divine Lord: (1) "*Between you and him alone.*" Although the Sisters, especially the younger ones and those who are not in office, should be very reserved and abstain from correcting faults on all occasions, and according to their fancy—for this would be prejudicial to themselves—nevertheless, let them practice charity toward one another, and give warnings and admonitions in a spirit of gentleness and discretion, especially when a Sister falls repeatedly into a fault which, though light, may entail serious consequences, as also when the fault is notable, but secret.

The Sisters are exhorted to receive the correction, whatever it may be, in a spirit of humility, tranquillity and silence—never yielding to trouble or to angry feelings against those who have admonished them. If the correction savors of malice, indiscretion, or evident falseness, there would often be virtue in not replying at the moment—rather suffering the charge in silence. They may, however, answer calmly that the case is not as it has been represented — or beg to consider the matter before God, in order to divest themselves of human considerations and to be enabled to speak and judge more accurately.

The second method of correction is that which is given before the Superioress or her Council, in accordance with these words of Christ: "*Take with you one, two, or three witnesses.*" This should be done when the fault is of consequence and not secret, or when, after having been privately admonished, the offender still persists in her failing. There are certain cases when it is unnecessary to reprove privately, and when the fault should be promptly manifested to the Superioress, so as to guard against scandal and serious consequences. The Sisters must know that they are never guilty of detraction in manifesting the faults of others to the Superioress, provided there is reason for so doing, and that they be not actuated by malice or ill-will; because they should trust to her prudence. When this method of correction is employed, the delinquent must silently submit to the penance ordained by the Rev. Mother and her Council.

The third manner of correction is practiced in full Chapter, or in presence of the whole Community. This is done, either when the offender makes her own accusation, or when the Mother Superioress or other Sisters, of whom there must be at least three, accuse some one of a serious fault. This measure is to be adopted when there is no amendment after private admonitions —even though the fault may not be known to the Community; hence, with greater reason, when the matter is public. The Mother Superioress' testimony, having a Sister as witness, should be believed in Chapter—and she who is thus convicted, should not dispute or make any reply, except it be to humble herself. If she fails on this point, the Superioress shall enforce silence in virtue of holy Obedience, and command her to remain prostrated until told to rise. Another Sister may perform some humiliation by way of mediation, and even ask to perform some penance for the guilty one. Should a Sister prove altogether refractory, and refuse to obey or submit to the penance imposed in Chapter, let no one venture to intercede in her behalf; rather, let all keep aloof, to humble her; but if this does not prove effectual, the whole Community should offer prayers and mortifications — such as prostrations, fasts, etc., for the poor rebellious and disobedient Sister, who will doubtless be covered with confusion at seeing the Community thus afflicted on her account. If, however, notwithstanding all this, she will not humble herself, let her be deprived of her black veil and ordered to withdraw into a separate room, debarred from all the exercises of the Community. Her meals are to be brought to her, and no one shall be allowed to speak to her, even so much as "*yes*" or "*no*," except the one appointed by the Superioress, who may, moreover, enjoin whatever penance she thinks proper.

INSTRUCTION.

God is at the same time so kind and so powerful, that He draws good out of our very-miseries. He permits us to commit faults every day, in order that we may become humble and glorify Him by our progress in His grace; for, our humiliation is frequently more agreeable to God, and honors Him more than our sins have dishonored Him. It is the easiest and most appropriate remedy — and is, in fact, the very one God demands of us. Accordingly, Chapters have been instituted in Religious Houses, to give us an occasion of humbling ourselves before God and the Community; to satisfy His Justice in some degree; to rise from our faults, renew ourselves in fervor, correct our ordinary failings, and to take strong and efficacious resolutions in the love and service of God.

When the Superioress is obliged to impose a severe penalty for serious offenses, such as have been mentioned above, let her beg our Lord to infuse into her heart the sweetness and efficacy of divine Charity.

For, though on the one hand, she should ever manifest a maternal heart in correcting, as well as in encouraging the Sisters, divesting herself of all passion, anger, and animosity; yet, on the other hand she must be filled with zeal for the glory of God and the good of Religion — fearing lest God withdraw His blessing and punish the Community for the neglected faults of individuals. On these occasions, let her imitate God's manner of dealing with His creatures, for He ever tempers Justice with Mercy. She should, however, always show herself more indulgent toward those who confess their faults and ask pardon for them; at the same time, let her be very firm and severe towards arrogant, malicious and obstinate members—never pardoning them until they have humbled themselves.

CHAPTER VII.

The Administration of Temporal Concerns, and the Chapter of Business Transactions.

There should be a safe with three keys in which all receipts exceeding one hundred dollars are to be deposited. One of the keys shall be kept by the Superioress, another by the Assistant, and the third by the Treasurer. In the safe there should be an account-book, in which are to be recorded all the amounts received, together with the date, the name of the donors, and the objects for which they have been received; and when, by the Mother Superioress' order, any sum is taken from this safe, the fact should likewise be noted in the same book, together with the date and the cause. Both the Treasurer and the Housekeeper should sign the statement of the expenses.

The Superioress must not decide or undertake anything of importance without the advice of her Council—of whom we shall make mention in treating of the various offices. Besides these, she should endeavor to find some influential and intelligent seculars—persons of known probity, and if possible, some lawyer or magistrate, whom she ought to consult in doubtful and intricate business matters—and their opinion should not be disregarded without serious reasons.

All the Sisters who have completed three years of profession shall assist at the Chapter of Business Affairs.

The Mother Superioress should convoke this assembly whenever it is necessary, or when circumstances require it. It shall be held at least twice a year; after Easter, and on the 13th of October, eight days before St. Ursula's feast, to lay before the Community the state of affairs.

The accounts of the receipts and expenses of the year (which shall have been read in council a few days previous), including those of the Housekeeper and of the Treasurer—all active and passive debts, all business transactions, contracts—in a word, every notable transaction of the year shall be here reported, the information being taken from the items furnished by the Superioress, the Treasurer and the Housekeeper, who should each keep a memorandum of what concerns her office in such a manner that all may be presented at the Pastoral Visitation. If there is anything to be changed or corrected, or if there are any orders to be given, it should be done in this Chapter.

The Superioress is obliged to assemble this Chapter for the Reception of Postulants to the holy Habit—as also when there is question of constructing new buildings, of making changes that materially alter the appearance of a house; the entire demolition of an edifice, and all notable contracts for the purchase, transfer, or exchange of property, the acceptance of foundations and perpetual obligations, etc. All other matters are to be treated in the council of the Rev. Mother Superioress.

After saying the "*Veni Sancte Spiritus,*" and all the Sisters being seated, the Superioress, or the Treasurer, shall lay down the propositions of the business in question. This should be done methodically—item after item; if another Sister has something to suggest, let her ask permission to do so, or else give her points to the Rev. Mother or to the Treasurer. Those who make any propositions may state their reasons *pro* and *con*, but without exaggeration or passion, that the affair may remain equally balanced. No one is permitted to interrupt another, or to speak out of her time, without a special permission — excepting the Superioress or the one who presides. These should commence by asking the opinion of the elder members present, allowing each one to say whatever she wishes. All should express their views briefly and with modesty and respect. After all have given their opinion, the Mother Superioress shall collect the votes and decide by the majority. The decisions should be carried out in full, and recorded by the Secretary of the Chapter, in the "Book of the Councils and Chapters."

If the affair requires more mature deliberation, the Chapter may adjourn. The secrecy of these assemblies must be inviolably preserved.

INSTRUCTION.

The mismanagement of temporal affairs causes ruin and disorder in the spiritual; whereas, if the former are well regulated and prudently managed, this will greatly contribute to the spiritual progress and government of the Community. The beautiful order established by divine Wisdom, shows that we are not to prefer earth to Heaven, the body to the soul, and perishable to eternal treasures; but rather that we should use the former to make ourselves worthy of the latter. God having bestowed them as means to coöperate in the sanctification and salvation of His elect, we must not frustrate His designs by an unlawful use of them—making household management and economy our principal care—thus insensibly permitting a spirit of covetousness and eagerness for temporal goods to glide into the Monastery; a disposition all the more dangerous as it appears so innocent, disguised as it is under the specious pretext of the general welfare. This would ultimately cause the Religious Vocation to be weighed in the balance with gold and silver; and the most expert managers would be considered the best Superioresses; the only care would be to economize wisely; the spirit of prayer would be replaced by speculations for the acquisition or the preservation of temporal goods, and the observance of many Rules would depend entirely on the expenses involved.

On the other hand, it is most important to avoid disorder, profuseness, superfluous expenses, and carelessness or want of diligence in the management of the funds, for this would occasion numberless troubles: debts and compromises, irregularities and private ownership among the Sisters—in a word, the ruin of peace and of the Religious spirit. These are the consequences of privations to which the Sisters are forcibly subjected, and of which they are not charitably relieved. Such conduct would finally compel them to have recourse to their relatives, or secretly keep things in reserve. To guard against these two opposite evils, the Sisters should consider that the property of the Community does not belong to them; hence, they should not become attached to it as their own possession. They are but the agents and dispensers of the same, and should, therefore, manage it carefully as ecclesiastical property and the patrimony of our divine Saviour, to whom they shall have to render an account, not only of the talents they have received in the order of grace and of their vocation, but also of their administration of temporal affairs.

Charity should reign in the heart of each member of the Community as queen of all the virtues; actuated by the spirit of charity, they should carefully provide for all the wants of the Sisterhood—in health, as well as in sickness; for their food, as well as for their raiment—in fact, their necessities should be even foreseen. The Sisters, on their part, animated by the spirit of poverty, should ever be content with what is given them, avoiding all murmurs and complaints. Let them love poverty and simplicity in everything, and ask for nothing but what is necessary in food and clothing—sacrificing all superfluities, and even showing themselves willing, often to endure the want of necessaries.

As God is in the midst of assemblies gathered in His name, the Sisters should assist at them with great reverence and attention—imagining they see our Saviour in their midst, and always referring to His glory whatever they may have to say or discuss.

CHAPTER VIII.

On the Reception and Training of Novices.

The Choir Sisters should not exceed forty in number, except for very important reasons, and when the Chapter decides that the good of the Monastery requires it. In this case, two more may be added to the number specified.

When a young lady presents herself as an aspirant, the Mother Superioress, with the advice of her Assistant and the Mistress of Novices, may receive her into the House, having previously requested the Assistant, the Mistress of Novices, and others she thinks proper, to see the young lady in the parlor from time to time, in order to test her vocation. She is to enter the Monastery dressed as a secular, and remain for three months as a boarder, that the Sisters may become acquainted with her. Meanwhile, the Superioress may occasionally allow her to come to the Community and assist at the Exercises, as may be judged proper. In her other duties, let her remain under the supervision of the Directress of the Academy. The Rev. Mother, with the consent of her Council, may dispense those she thinks proper from this first trial. The aspirants should be dressed in modest attire, and present themselves from time to time to the Superioress, the Assistant and the Mistress of Novices—humbly begging the favor of being admitted into the Novitiate.

The holy Habit should, as a general rule, not be given before the completion of the seventeenth year. It suffices, however, for its validity, that the profession be made at the completion of the eighteenth year. No one shall be admitted to receive the Religious Habit, or to make their profession, except by the plurality of votes given by all the Sisters assembled in Chapter. To insure greater freedom, the votes are to be given by means of black and white beans: the white denoting admission, the black, rejection. Each Sister must be given one of each kind, that she may cast into the box the one she chooses, without its being perceived by any one else.

As the greatest evil that could befall a Community, is to receive members without a vocation, the Sisters should be very careful in giving their votes for the Vesture; but let them be even more cautious for the profession—for after this, they are obliged to retain and support those whom they have admitted. Hence, they should never allow temporal interests or human considerations of friendship or relationship to bias their decisions. As a precaution on this head, near relatives, including those of the second degree, namely: the aunts and first cousins of the Postulants, or Novices, shall have no voice for them, and they must retire from the Chapter-room while the votes are being given. This rule applies even to the Superioress.

It is never allowed to receive persons who have contagious diseases, or such as have lost the use of their limbs to such a degree, that they would be incapable of performing any of the functions of the Religious life. The Community should rarely admit sick, infirm, one-eyed or lame persons, or such as have any notable physical deformity, unless they have eminent qualities of mind and of virtue, which may compensate for these defects; or else, if they be founders or signal benefactors.

Let the Sisters be extremely careful as to the mental qualities of aspirants—never admitting idiotic or melancholy persons, or such as are subject to intervals of insanity, or who give evidence of a malicious or violent disposition, or any other vice for which there is no hope of amendment. They should never receive such as have been publicly stigmatized with infamy, persons who are betrothed or married, or who are involved in debt—requiring that this debt be first paid, or that the consent of the creditors be obtained. Finally, they should not admit young persons who are necessary to their parents; and as rarely as possible without the consent and blessing of the parents. Poverty should not be considered a reason for exclusion; on the contrary, if the House is endowed, and able to bear the expense, it would be advisable to admit occasionally, persons without means, provided they have in other respects, the requisite qualifications.

The Community should, however, ordinarily insist on the dowry, for the support and maintenance of the House; yet the Chapter should never take this into consideration in casting their votes—weighing, above all things, the aspirant's vocation and dispositions of piety.

More than two Sisters of one family should not be received in the same House except for weighty reasons, of which the Bishop is to be notified.

When a Sister receives the Habit, a name of devotion shall be added to that of her Baptism instead of the surname by which she was known in the world, and which she drops—that, together with her name, she may *"forget her people and her father's house."*

The probation of Novices shall last an entire year. In case of infirmity, or for other important reasons, this time may be prolonged.

The Novices shall assist with the Community at all the Offices, Meditations, and Common Prayers; at the Refectory Recreations, and at Chapter, from which they must, however, withdraw, after having been the first to make their accusations. They should also assist at the Conference and Spiritual Reading, from 4 to 5 P. M. on Sundays and festivals. Their other exercises shall be performed separately, and their apartments should be separated from the rest, especially from those of the Boarders, with whom they shall have no communication. In winter they should have their fire apart. No Sister is permitted to amuse herself with the Novices, or to speak to them, except with permission and during the Recreation, or when occupied with them in the same employment, much less is it allowed for the Novices to visit and converse with the Sisters, without leave from their Mistress. All should be careful to edify the Novices, never acting with too much freedom in their presence—for our Lord hurls His maledictions agains those who scandalize His little ones—with all the more reason, as young souls are more susceptible to good or bad impressions.

Let each Novice have a Journal, or an extract of the daily Regulations—interior as well as exterior—which the Mistress shall have read in the Novitiate once a week, explaining some point thereof, or giving any other pious instruction she may deem suitable for Novices.

On Wednesdays they shall make their accusations before their Mistress, and humbly receive the mortifications and penances she may impose. Let her grant them some innocent recreations, but, above all things, let her endeavor, as much as possible, to banish Melancholy from the Novitiate.

About the end of the year of probation the Novices shall present themselves three times at Chapter, and kneeling, humbly solicit to be admitted to the Religious Profession. When there is no Chapter for business transactions they may present themselves at that of the Accusations. The year being completed, if they have been received, they shall make their solemn Profession according to the form prescribed in the Ceremonial. Their Profession, together with the date thereof, must be recorded in a book and signed by themselves.

The Novices are, during the three years following their Profession, excluded from the right of voting and of membership in Chapter. Meanwhile let them remain in the Novitiate, practising the Rules and Observances under the direction of the Mistress of Novices, unless the Mother Superioress, with the advice of the Spiritual Director, withdraw them before the end of the specified term, for some reasonable cause. This custom is observed in honor and imitation of the Apostles, who were three years under the guidance and direction of our Lord, before they received the Holy Spirit, or exercised any functions in His Church.

INSTRUCTION.

The grace of the Religious life is a treasure of inestimable value, and most worthy of being desired and sought with zeal and labor by those whom God calls thereunto. This grace should be received with humility and gratitude, and preserved and perfected with fervor and fidelity. Hence, there is nothing so important in Religion as the discernment of vocations and the proper direction of Novices. This is accomplished in the Novitiate, where, as in a sacred nursery, these young plants take root and strengthen themselves in their calling—growing and advancing each day in grace, and receiving from God, by means of the instructions that are given them, the bent, the impressions, and the dispositions which they retain, as a general rule, throughout their whole life.

Accordingly, there are three things to be weighed and considered on this subject; namely, the admission of young persons into Religion, their training in the Novitiate and their reception to the Religious Profession. Remembering that our Lord was pleased, for our instruction, to watch all night in prayer on the mountain, before choosing His Apostles, and that notwithstanding all this, there was one among them, who, by a terrible, but equitable judgment, fell from the Apostolate and was lost. With how much greater reason should the Sisters have recourse to prayer, and never admit a new member without careful examination and mature reflection. Let them earnestly recommend this matter to our Lord and His Blessed Mother, and offer at least one Holy Communion for this intention. If there is any case in which they should imitate the firm and gentle Spirit of Jesus, it should be especially in this, where mercy and compassion for a certain individual, might often prove a species of cruelty towards the Community. On the other hand, however, they should rely on the kind Providence of God, for if, after recommending the matter to Him, and offering a general Communion for this end, the Sisters proceed, with a good intention, purely for God's glory, and according to the dictates of their conscience, He will be with them, and will not permit them to be mistaken in the decisions of the Chapter. For this reason they should contemplate and honor Him as ever present—directing His Church, and in it, their own little Community, by the presence and assistance of His Holy Spirit.

CHAPTER IX.

The Lay Sisters.

The number of Lay Sisters should, as a general rule, not exceed the fourth of that of the Choir-nuns. They should have a good constitution, be healthy and strong in body, of an humble mind, docile, tractable and indifferent to all kinds of labor and employment.

They should be made to wait six months before entering the Novitiate. During this interval let them take their meals in the place assigned by the Superioress, and assist at one of the Exercises, Conferences or Spiritual Readings, as the Mistress of Novices may judge proper. At the end of this term they may be admitted into the Novitiate as Postulants, wearing the secular dress a year, at the end of which they may receive the Habit of a Novice. The year following they may make their Profession in the same manner as the Choir Novices, if they are judged fit. The Mistress of Novices should provide for them as well as for the others, instructing them in the spirit of their vocation, and training them in the practice of religious virtues.

The Lay Sisters should never be called to the Chapter for business transactions of the Monastery, which pertains exclusively to the Choir Sisters; neither should they assist in the Choir, among those who psalmody the office; but they may attend this Holy Exercise in the Tribune, or kneeling behind the benches of the Choir-nuns. Let them entertain a particular respect for the Choir Sisters, who should love and cherish them as Sisters, and treat them with Religious Charity.

The Lay Sisters are to be under the supervision of the Housekeeper, and all should learn how to cook. Let the Mistress of Novices, or any other whom the Superioress may appoint, attend to their advancement in virtue, see to their Spiritual Reading, and on Sundays and festivals, teach them the Catechism, and how to practise the virtues of Religious life. Let her also visit them from time to time, in their employments, instruct them how to work religiously, and prove herself a charitable Mother in all their wants and necessities.

INSTRUCTION.

Let nothing be considered little in the House of God, since all is consecrated to the service of so great a Majesty, or tends to promote His glory. All greatness in Religion consists in true humility and charity, for, according to the words of life, she who wishes to be the greatest must become the least, and she who is the first must be the servant of the others. Hence, the condition of the Lay Sisters should not be regarded as a servile state of contempt and abjection, but rather as a vocation, similar to that which fell to the lot of the devoted Martha, who was busy and eager in honoring and serving her good Master. He, Himself, declares that He will consider as done to Himself whatever we do to the least of His servants.

As members of one body, each of which has its own special functions, let the Sisters in the various employments, conditions and degrees, be animated by the same spirit, strive after the same end, participate in the same graces, and await the same recompense at the last day—the fruit of their united labors in the same vineyard of Religion. This will be the crown of glory which the Just Judge and Father of Mercy will award to each, according to the degree of her fidelity and her merit in grace.

CHAPTER X.

On the Lodging, Reception and Instruction of the Boarders.

The dwelling destined for the boarders' lodging should be separate from the Monastery, and, as much as possible, have no means of access, either up or down stairs, to the regular places of the Community. These must always be kept locked, and should never be opened except by the Sisters in charge of the Boarders; and they must never allow the children to open them.

The Superioress, only, has the power to admit the Boarders, and, in case of sickness, this right devolves on the Assistant. Let none be received below seven or over eighteen years of age, except for very particular reasons, and with the advice of the Council and of the Director or Confessor. Great care should be taken that the Boarders be modestly dressed and properly accommodated, so that all in the House of God may be suggestive of Christian Piety.

Among the Sisters charged with the care and instruction of the Boarders, there should be a Superintendent over the others, whose duty it is to take care of the pupils' money, clothing and furniture. She should provide for all their necessities of which she must keep a faithful account, so as to be able to present a correct statement of their expenses. The Children must alway be guarded by one of the Sisters, who should never allow them to be out of sight, except it be for a short time.

As the principal end of this Institution is the love of our Neighbor, and includes the instruction of young girls, the Sisters should teach their pupils all that their condition requires them to know, instilling at the same time, the spirit of piety and truly christian sentiments. Hence, those who are charged with their instruction should be particularly careful to teach them the Mysteries of our Holy Faith, embodied in the Apostles Creed; the object of the principal Feasts celebrated by the Church; the manner of approaching the Sacraments, and of saying their prayers, as specified in the Book of Customs.

The Sisters should faithfully correct them of their faults, and endeavor to excite them to the love of God, and of solid virtue.

The pupils shall be taught to read, write, sew, and how to do all kinds of needle-work and useful labor, that may be deemed necessary for their condition. It is permitted to engage secular teachers — whether male or female — to give lessons in vocal and instrumental music, in drawing, etc.

CHAPTER XI.

The Young Ladies' Day-School, and the Sunday-School.

Besides the School House in which the Boarders are taught, there should be a separate apartment for the Day Scholars, who come in the morning and return home in the evening. This should be easy of access from without, so that the children may enter without passing through the Monastery gate. The inner, as well as the outer doors of this department should be well locked, and never opened except by one of the Portresses, by a Teacher, or some other whom the Superioress may appoint. The inner doors may be opened three-quarters or half an hour before school opens; the outer ones only when the children are to enter. If possible, there should be a convenient place adjoining or near the class rooms, where all the scholars may assemble before school opens; and there should be a grating, to which one of the Teachers should go from time to time to see that they behave properly.

No pupils should be admitted under the age of six. Let the Boarders have no communication with the Day Scholars, nor the Day Scholars with the Boarders, or with the interior of the Monastery. The Sisters should rejoice in our Lord, and take a peculiar delight in teaching poor children, thus honoring the mission of our blessed Saviour, who, as the Prophet tells us, was sent *to evangelize the poor*. They should, therefore, refuse no child on account of poverty; but these may be separated from the others, as the rudeness which is common among persons of this class might prove prejudicial to children of good family; and also because the poor require plainer instruction.

The Day Scholars, as well as the Boarders, must be taught their prayers and all the obligations of a Christian life. For this end, let them be assembled every Sunday, Thursday and feast day Let the Sisters zealously devote themselves to this duty, as it is the principal object of their vocation.

An instruction should be given on the Sundays and Festivals specified by the

Superioress, at which both women and children may assist, but no men. On these days the doors are to remain closed until it is time for the instruction. The place where the Sister gives the instruction must be separated from that of the outsiders by means of a grating, through which she may hear the day-scholars recite; the Boarders remain with her, in the enclosure. This custom should be carefully preserved as the primitive spirit by means of which this Order has produced great fruit from its very foundation. The Sister charged with this office must speak of nothing but what is contained in the Catechism — adding some familiar examples illustrative of the mysteries which every Christian should know, and some useful instructions on the practice of virtue. Let the Mother Superioress appoint the most prudent and competent among the Sisters, for the exercise of this charge.

INSTRUCTION.

The beauty of the Spouse of the Heavenly King, that is to say, the Church, displays itself in the charming and agreeable variety of her Religious Orders and Societies, each of which has its own vocation, its peculiar customs, and its divers functions,—performed, as the Apostle expresses it, in one manner or another, yet, it is the same Spirit which operates all in all. The least among these Orders is that of the Ursulines, who are destined, not only to work at their own perfection and salvation, but also to aid and benefit their neighbor by the instruction of young girls, who they are to train from their tenderest years in the fear and love of God, conducting them in the way of eternal salvation, nurturing these young plants of their sex—so that hereafter, they may people cities and spread the good seed of piety that has been sown in their own hearts; or on the other hand, that those whom God calls to a more exalted perfection in some Religious Order of the Church, may render themselves worthy of their vocation. Thus not only society in general, but even Monasteries will reap the friuts of this Institute. The former, as well as the latter, having served God according to the requirements of their state and condition, shall one day, by the grace and mercy of God, be numbered among the Elect.

This vocation is sublime, and should be valued and highly esteemed by those whom God calls thereunto. Its office is that of the good Angels who are charged with the care of souls; nay, it even possesses an advantage over the heavenly spirits—for a single Angel is appointed to guard a single soul, and this, by means that are secret, hidden and invisible; whereas a single Religious may direct many by means that are exterior, sensible, and proportioned to the simplicity of children—thus coöperating in the realization of their eternal predestination. This should not astonish us, for, since the Incarnation of His Son, God has raised man above the Angels, to aid and coöperate in the work of grace. He sent, not Angels, but twelve poor fishermen, to preach His Gospel throughout His world, and He wishes man to be conducted and saved by man.

The life of Ursulines should not, therefore, be wholly contemplative—devoted to self in retreat and solitude; neither should it be purely active, exclusively devoted to works of charity, but mixed and solidly grounded in prayer and the love of God, so that others may share the plenitude of this love.

The Sisters should be all the more given to contemplation, as they are to draw from this source grace and light, not only for themselves, but also for the benefit of others, inasmuch as their sex and condition will allow. This office which they embrace in behalf of their neighbor is not merely one of charity or of mercy like that of the Hospitallers and other similar congregations, which are peculiarly the vocation of Lay Sisters; but rather and principally, to labor for the salvation of souls and in works of grace. This object, being very exalted, requires excellent dispositions, namely: purity of intention, perfect self sacrifice, an ardent love for God, disinterested zeal for the salvation of souls, and all the virtues and dispositions which establish a good Religious in evangelical perfection; for no one can give what he does not possess—and one must exist before he can act. That is to say the Sisters must be in a state of eminent grace before they can operate and produce the effects of grace in souls.

There is a vast difference between embracing some great employment and applying oneself thereto by the spirit of vocation and of grace, and performing the same through inclination, charity or other motives when it is not precisely an obligation of our state in life. Hence, it is very important that the Ursulines should know and understand that they are called to instruct youth; that this is their vocation, and that God will give them grace to acquit themselves worthily of this duty. Let them enter into this spirit from the very beginning of their Religious life, and awaken in themselves a desire to work with ardor in the field of their vocation, purely for the glory and love of God.

CHAPTER XII.

The Pastoral Visitation.

This Visitation may take place once every year, and should be made once at least every three years. The Ursulines, being under the jurisdiction of the Ordinaries of the places where the Monasteries are established, to these belong the right and authority to make the Visitation in person, or to authorize another to make it in their name. However, if they cannot come in person, let them be respectfully solicited to delegate the one whom the Superioress and the Chapter may propose, and to be pleased to restrict the authority of said delegate, limiting it to an inspection of the manner in which the Rules and Constitutions are observed, and to the reformation and prohibition of whatever may be contrary to good morals, to piety and to Religious Modesty.

The Sisters are bound in conscience, and the Visitor may oblige them under certain penalties, to make known to him all that they believe to be done contrary to the Rules and Constitutions, or whatever they may consider prejudicial to Religious life. They should speak with sincerity, and not wilfully change or disguise any fact.

INSTRUCTION.

The Son of God descended from on High to visit us in His mercy, as Zachary expresses it in his Canticle. This, His visit, should be honored by that which is made in Religious houses, in accordance with the Council of Trent. The object of the Ecclesiastical visitation is to draw a visit from the Holy Ghost into our souls, to correct, reform and destroy the old Adam with all his works, and to renew us in Jesus Christ, the new Adam, created according to God. This external visitation performed by ecclesiastical authority, unaccompanied by the interior, which is effected by grace and the renovation of spirit, would be only a ceremony similar to those of the old Law, which had no power to sanctify. The principal fruit of the visit should be a reformation, not only of the exterior, but especially of the interior—that is to say, a true renovation of spirit.

Hence, all the Sisters in general, and each one in particular, should prepare for this visitation by an interior renovation, which they should ask from the Father of Mercy. Let them offer this exterior visit to that of the Son of God in coming into this world; to the interior visit of the Holy Spirit, replenishing souls with His graces; and to the last and terrible visit of our divine Lord at the general judgment. Let them dispose themselves for the first, by adoration and profound humility; for the second, by a renewal of fervor and love; and for the third, by a sincere desire to persevere until death in the fear and love of God.

By endeavoring to combine these various dispositions in their soul, they will merit to receive the grace and enjoy the effects of these three visits.

END OF PART II.

PART III.

Treating of the Various Offices in the Community and of the Interior Dispositions required for the proper discharge of the duties they involve.

CHAPTER I.

General Dispositions for the Offices in the Monastery.

The Queen of Sheba, having heard of the wisdom of Solomon, came from a distant country, to witness with her own eyes the good order and wise government of his household. But when she saw that the reality incomparably exceeded the renown, she exclaimed in a transport of admiration: *Oh! how happy are the servants who are daily before thee and who hear thy wisdom.*

Now what shall we say of the glorious orders of the celestial hierarchy, composed of so many myriads of blessed spirits, who minister and assist before the Majesty of God, each according to his rank and office; the special functions of his ministry being distinct from those of all the other angels, and assigned him by the Divine Providence and Eternal Wisdom, according to his degree and the elevation of his nature in God.

Religious Houses that are well regulated have doubtless an advantage over the household of the Wise Man, inasmuch as the King whom they serve is greater than Solomon. *"And behold a greater than Solomon,"* says this same King and Saviour. The Sisters should, therefore, as far as human weakness allows, imitate the divine and admirable order of the Celestial Court. Indeed, if we were not oppressed by the weight of our mortal bodies, we would, like the Angels, require none but spiritual means for our guidance. But, in this lowly state of our earthly existence, we need laws and rules to guide us, to mark the distinction between the various Offices, and to point out the duties they impose.

Each official should apply herself to her charge with the three following dispositions: (1) Obedience and submission towards God, accepting the employment from His Hand and by His Order, and performing it with actual dependence on His holy Will. (2) Fidelity in regard to others, acquitting herself of her duties with exactitude—not failing in anything, remembering that her work is the work of God. (3) Purity of intention in regard to herself, divesting herself of all attachments and repugnances, ordinarily suggested by self-love, and applying herself to the duties of her office from the pure motive of the love of God.

The three following objects of devotion and piety may be suggested in general to all the officials: (1) The holy and adorable Providence of God which extends its care to the least objects—to a hair of our head, to a leaf of a tree, and to the smallest insect. (2) The Word Incarnate, who united Himself personally to our human nature with all its attributes, each of which is filled, sanctified, and deified by the Divinity. (3) The real Presence of the

Sacred Humanity of our Lord Jesus, who sees all our actions, even the most hidden and insignificant. These considerations will enable the Sisters to attend faithfully to everything that belongs to their charge.

Let them adore in their duties the eternal Providence of God, which acts in all the events of life. Let them ask grace to perfect and sanctify all their exterior actions in union with, and in honor of, those performed by the Man-God. Finally, let them endeavor to have Him always before their eyes, and to perform all their duties in His presence, saying and practising what the Psalmist expresses: *"As the eyes of the servant are on the hands of his master; and as the eyes of the handmaid are on the hands of her mistress, so are our eyes fixed on God, our Lord."*

CHAPTER II.

The Election and Inauguration of the Mother Superioress and Other Officers.

The election of a Superioress and an Assistant shall take place every three years, on an appointed day within the octave of St. Ursula's Feast. They cannot be elected for more than three years, nor continue in office longer than six years at a time, under pain of nullity. The Superioress must, however, continue in office until the new elections shall have been made and confirmed. The Chapter may elect a Superioress and an Assistant from another House of this Institute of the Presentation, provided the desired Sisters be not in office or necessary to their respective Communities, and that this be in accordance with the good pleasure of the Rt. Rev. Bishops. Communities should thus mutually assist one another, as has always been done hitherto; but, the time of their office having expired, these Sisters should return to their House of Profession.

The Sisters should receive Holy Communion on the three days preceding the Elections, for this intention, and each day, recite the "*Veni Creator*" after Mass. The Spiritual Director, or in his absence, the Father Confessor, should notify the Community that on such a day, after the holy Sacrifice of Mass and Holy Communion, the election of a Superioress and an Assistant is to take place. If he thinks proper, he may add a few words, exhorting the Sisters to divest themselves of all self-interest, that they may receive light from God to direct them in so important an action. During these days, all the Sisters, including the Novices and Lay-Sisters, should perform some extra devotions, to implore God's assistance. If it can be conveniently done, let the B. Sacrament be exposed during two hours, that the Sisters may, in turn, pray before it, for this intention. Let them imitate Jesus, who teaches us by His example, how to prepare for a good and holy Election; for, when about to choose His twelve Apostles, He withdrew to a mountain and there spent the whole night in prayer, taking His resolutions with God, His Father.

Let the Sisters form no plots and make neither direct or indirect efforts to be elected to any charge, nor speak on this subject at recreation, in assemblies, or elsewhere, by way of intrigue in favor of themselves or others. If there are any surprised in, and convicted of such a fault, this having been proved by the testimony of three Sisters on oath, the delinquents are to be deprived of the right of both active and passive votes at the present Election, and even for one, two, or three years, according to the decision of the retiring Superioress and her Council.

The qualities of the Superioress-elect should be more than angelical, since, according to the expression of the Council of Trent, she is called to direct Angels on earth. She should be forty years of age and eight years professed, or at least, thirty years old and five years professed; but in cases of necessity, the Bishop may grant a dispensation on this subject. The Sister chosen for this position should be of an amiable, condescending character;—one who has conformed to the regulations of the Community and who is able to enforce their observance and to treat of business matters. Nevertheless, special care should be taken that the Elect possess such piety as to be of service to the Sisters in their spiritual direction; in a word, let the Sisters choose the one most eminent in fervor, stability of character, zeal and patience.

The Election is made by ballots or secret votes in the choir—the grating being open—and in presence of the Rt. Rev. Bishop, or of the Spiritual Director or any other Clergyman whom the Bishop may judge proper to appoint, to preside and confirm the Elections in his name. An election is canonical only when more than half the votes are given for the same person; for instance, of twenty, one must have eleven, of nineteen, ten; of twenty-one, eleven, &c. If, however, after the first or second ballot, an election cannot be made, no one having the required majority, the third ballot decides by the plurality of votes, and the one who has the most, although it be not the half, shall be considered rightly and canonically elected. In case any two Sisters have an equal number, the elder Professed is elected.

On the third day, after Mass, the "*Veni Creator*" having been sung, the one who presides may, if he thinks proper, deliver a short exhortation. Hereupon, the Sisters who have no active voice retire; the Superioress kneels before the Celebrant, and having briefly accused herself of the faults she has committed during her administration, asks a penance together with her discharge and the election of another in her place. This having been granted with whatever penance the Celebrant may think proper to impose, she goes to a small table near the grating, and after making the sign of the Cross, writes on a small piece of paper, simply the name of the one to whom she wishes to give her vote, and nothing else, not even her signature, so that no one either from within or without may see what she has written or to whom she has given her vote. Having folded the paper and cast it into the box held by the Celebrant, she retires and takes her seat in the last place, after all the others. Hereupon, the Assistant advances to write and cast her vote, after which she returns to her place; the same is done by each of the others in turn.

In case there are any too sick to come to the Choir, the Celebrant should depute two of the older Sisters to go and collect their votes, which should if possible, be written by the sick in person, so that it may not be known for whom they have voted. However, if they are not able to write, they may choose any Sister they please to write their vote for them; this being folded, is to be brought to the Choir and cast into the box. The one who presides may go in person to collect the votes of the sick, if such be his desire.

All the votes having been cast, the Celebrant, assisted by the Father Confessor or another Priest who shall have accompanied him, opens the box in the presence of the Sisters, and counts the votes. Let the Assistant and the Sacristan, on their side, count the Sisters having active votes, and see that the ballot corresponds. Should there be less or more votes than Sisters, the ballot is null and must be re-commenced. This done, the votes are opened, read, and carefully counted by the Celebrant and his assistants, as also by the Sisters in the choir, marking each vote with a stroke of the pen. When it becomes necessary to have recourse to another ballot, the one who presides should first cause the former votes to be burnt at the grating; in presence of all the Sisters; but when an election has been made, he replaces the votes in the box and declares the result, saying: "*Adjutorium nostrum in Nomine Domini*," to which the choir responds, "*Qui fecit ceolum et terram;* whereupon he adds: "*Sister N—has been "elected to be Superioress of this Community, "to govern it according to God, the Constitu- "tions, and her conscience. The whole number "of votes in the Community being N—N are "for her election, and this is a sufficient num- "ber. Now, if any Sister know of any legiti- "mate and canonical obstacle, let her declare "it immediately; otherwise her testimony will "be neither received nor heard.*" After this let no objection be heeded that could render the Election doubtful or null, unless it be something positively evident; for instance, that the Elect had not been entitled to a passive vote,—or anything else of this nature. Having made a considerable pause, if no one speaks, the Sacristan rings the bell to assemble all the Sisters, including the

Novices and Lay-Sisters. When all are present, the Celebrant calls the Superioress-elect by name. She must rise promptly, and without saying a word to excuse or to humble herself, kneel before him while he says in a loud and distinct voice : *" Having " been authorized by our Rt. Rev. Bishop, to " assist at the present Election, we declare " that Mother N—has been legitimately and " canonically elected to be Superioress of this " House and Monastery of St. Ursula, of the " Presentation of our Lady ; and by the same " authority, we confirm said Election. " In the name of the Father and of the Son, and of the Holy Ghost."* Having made the sign of the Cross, he exhorts all the Sisters to accept, obey, and respect the Elect in her quality of Superioress ; and if he thinks proper, let him address her a few words. Hereupon, the Assistant and the retiring Superioress conduct the Superioress-elect to her official place, where they and each of the other Sisters in turn, kneel to salute her. Raising them, she gives to each the kiss of peace, while the choir sings the *" Te Deum"*

At the conclusion of the hymn, the Sisters who have no active voice, retire, and the Assistant advances, kneels before the Celebrant, accuses herself of the faults she has committed in her office, and begs to be discharged. The one who presides follows the same ceremonial as has been indicated for the election of the Superioress. The Assistant having taken the last place in the Choir, the Sisters cast their votes, which having been read and counted as before mentioned, the one having the plurality of votes is elected. In case two or three have the same number, let the oldest professed be considered legitimately elected without any other formality. The Celebrant having called her by name, she rises and, without a word of excuse, kneels before him while he says : " *Sister N— we declare that you have* " *been legitimately elected, to fill the office of* " *Assistant in this Monastery ; and by the* " *authority we have received, we hereby con-* " *firm your Election. In the name of the* " *Father, and of the Son, and of the Holy* " *Ghost, Amen.*" Hereupon the Superioress conducts her to the Assistant's place and embraces her. The same is done by all the

Sisters, including the Novices and Lay-Sisters, who shall have been summoned as mentioned above. Let them first salute the new Assistant with a profound bow which she returns, embracing all who present themselves.

The new Superioress may spend the three days immediately following the Elections, in retirement, recollecting herself in our Lord and offering to Him, her being, her new duties, the monastery, and the entire Community. During these days, she should have no communication with seculars, and the Sisters should be careful to leave her undisturbed. Let her during this time, reflect on the appointment of the different officials, and deliberate with the former Superioress and Assistant on this subject.

Let her assemble the Chapter, at the latest, eight days after her election, to elect a Treasurer and two Counsellors, this is done by the plurality of votes at a secret ballot. Besides the Assistant and the Treasurer, the Superioress may propose as Counsellors, those she thinks fit for this office, without, however, imposing any obligation on the Community to elect them.

It is for the Superioress and her Council to appoint all the other officers of the Community. These may be changed, and others nominated, whenever the Rev. Mother and her Council judge it expedient; and when such changes or new appointments are to be made, let the matter be proposed at the next Chapter.

INSTRUCTION.

We read in the Sacred Scriptures that the Holy Ghost separated Saul and Barnabas, to make use of each for the work for which he had been destined. In like manner, it is for Him to make choice of those whom He wishes to employ in the government, or in the various offices and employments of the Monastery. The votes and decisions of the Sisters should be considered only as the interpretation and manifestation of His will in regard to the Community.

If in these elections, on which depend the good order and government of the Community, the Sisters act with religious simplicity, purity of intention, and true zeal to preserve the spirit of piety and regularity in the Community; avoiding all intrigue, self-interest and murmuring, they may confide in the goodness and mercy of their common Father and Master, who by directing all their thoughts and votes, will Himself preside at the Elections, and give to those who have been chosen, the necessary light and strength to discharge the duties of their respective offices, and His paternal Providence will protect and sanctify all the members of the Community.

CHAPTER III.

The Mother Superioress.

The vigilance of the Mother Superioress should extend generally and particularly to all that concerns the Community, in spiritual as well as in temporal matters. Let her never consider anything beneath her notice and care, and as much as possible attend to matters personally. Let her watch and direct all the offices and charges; visit the Officials at least once a month, endeavoring to discover the faults that may be committed and whatever may require correction—never tolerating anything that is contrary to the Rules, Constitutions, and Customs. In case of sickness or other necessities of the Officials, she should supply their absence.

Every Sister should occasionally give an account of her charge to the Superioress, who should see that each accomplishes her duty with fidelity and exactitude.

The Rev. Mother should, if possible, speak to each of the Sisters once a month, in private, to learn the state of their souls, their progress in virtue, the obstacles and temptations they may experience—all of which, the Sisters should make known to her with filial confidence. For this end, let her receive them with a maternal heart full of charity,—showing herself ready to console, assist, and relieve all in their necessities—never disdaining any, even the least Sister in the House, for all, including the Lay-Sisters and even the Turn-Sisters are the servants of Jesus Christ. Hence, the Superioress should act towards all according to their capacity and requirements. The Novices should be visited even more frequently and with greater assiduity. Let the Superioress be careful in her interior, as well as exterior administration, not to limit herself to her own thoughts, sentiments and private opinions; but, rising superior to her own littleness, let her accommodate herself to the ways and views of others entering into their sentiments and subjecting herself to varying circumstances.

As the Superioress is to be the light and guide of others, she should instruct by her example, no less than by her words. Hence, let her observe in everything the general order of the Community, never privately attributing anything thereof to herself, nor permitting any exception, privilege or singularity in her favor, whether in her food, clothing, or in the furniture of her cell, except what may be necessary for her health, and to this, the charity of the Sisters may oblige her. Moreover, in order that she who guides others may herself live under direction, let the Mother Assistant take care of her and her wants; and the Superioress must obey her in all that regards herself personally.

The Rev. Mother should assist as punctually as possible at all the assemblies of the Choir, Refectory, Recreation, hours of manual labor; &c.; never dispensing herself without cause—thus honoring the Son of God in the midst of His Apostles, in a word, let her be exact at all the regular observances. On entering on her charge, and at certain times during each year, for instance during the Annual Retreat, the Superioress should occupy herself in the lower offices of the House; such as, serving in the kitchen, and the like, to imitate our Lord who began to work before He taught, and also, to teach others by her example, how much they should love these humiliating services.

She should carefully preserve peace as the most precious treasure of the Community; not only by promptly reconciling those who may be at variance and inducing them to ask one another's pardon without much questioning as to who is in the right;—but also by employing all the means that prudence may suggest, to check the aversions and secret alienations that may have arisen among the Sisters. Let her show them all an equal charity, never indulging in flattery, caresses, or weak complacence with some, or tolerating in herself any particular friendship, since she is bound to extirpate these in others; for such conduct on her part would be the ruin of true Charity.

As to what regards temporal matters, let the Superioress be very careful to see that the wants of the Sisters be all charitably supplied, always however, in accordance with Religious simplicity. This charity must extend especially to the sick, the infirm and the aged. She should examine if the Officials acquit themselves of their charges with charity and if the Sisters obey them. When privately informed of a fault that has been committed, let her examine the matter and prudently apply a remedy. She shall superintend the more important business transactions and take special precautions that the House be not involved in debt. She may dispose of the ordinary alms received at the door,—of what is left at table, and of cash, to the amount of three dollars a month, but not more without the advice of her Council. It is the duty of the Superioress to change when necessary, the Lawyer, Agent, Physician, Druggist, Grocer, Workmen, in a word, all seculars who may be engaged in the service of the Community.

INSTRUCTION.

We observe and honor two kinds of grace in our Lord, Jesus:—one is called the personal grace, which fills and sanctifies His sacred Humanity; the other is the primary, or essential grace, of the plenitude of which we have all received. Hence the Superioress, who holds the place of the Son of God in the Community, should ask a two-fold grace, a two-fold intelligence, a two fold heart, a two-fold light and a two-fold charity; one for herself individually, so as to advance and persevere in the ways of God, in the spirit of fear and humility. The other, to gain influence over souls and to serve for the guidance of the Community. It is to be remarked that this guidance is not according to nature, nor the effect of mere human prudence, or of a certain external policy, but rather the charge of souls called to a supernatural end—to the path of Religious perfection—souls who must consequently be directed by Divine light and grace. Moreover, as the Sisters are not subject to the Superioress, to be guided according to her private views, her passions, or her personal inclinations, but according to the spirit of God in her— let her forget herself, strip herself of her own affections and sentiments, and renounce her views, thus subjecting herself to the sovereignty and guidance of the Holy Spirit, in whom she should govern and direct those confided to her care. She may rest assured that in proportion as she reveres and submits herself to the direction of the Divine Spirit, He will cause those under her charge to respect and submit to her authority. Therefore, let all her care be—not to attract and bind souls to herself, but, rather, to lead and present them to our Lord, to whom they belong, and in whose name she must guard them as precious deposits. Finally, let her devote herself to the direction of souls and of the Community, not as to her own work or a task which she may appropriate to herself, but as to the "*work of our Lord Jesus Christ.*" Such is the doctrine of the Apostle.

The Superioress should accept the charge that has been legitimately imposed on her, without indulging either joy or sadness—refraining from fine words to excuse or apparently humble herself. As it is a responsibility which should be neither sought nor desired, let her accept it in silence, and with religious simplicity and humility, not as an honor on which to pride herself; not as an authority to domineer over others; not as a heavy burden under which to succumb; not as a forced and painful cross—filling her soul with sadness, disgust and weariness. Rather let her consider Superiority as our Lord's yoke, which is sweet and light; as a cross full of unction, and a charge full of grace, in which she should consider—not herself, but God, by whom it has been imposed. Thus, strengthened by the grace which the Almighty has attached to the position, and using it profitably, the burden of the office will not fill her soul with disgust, its honors will not cause her to become elated, nor its authority domineering. To this end the Superioress should, on entering her charge, begin by the humblest actions, and serve in the lowliest offices in the House, remembering our Saviour's words to St. John, when, before manifesting Himself to the world, He subjected Himself to receive the Baptism of a sinner, at the hands of His Precursor: "*It thus becometh us to fulfil all justice.*" That is to say, according to some of the Doctors, "to fulfil all humility."

In the exercise of her office the Superioress should be vigilant without eagerness; prompt but not precipitate, in executing projects that have been maturely considered; strong and efficacious in directing all things to their end; mild and gentle in her manner of action; yet stern and rigorous in preventing or reproving vice—particularly such as may be especially opposed to the Spirit of God in the Community—always, however, full of true charity and affability towards individuals. She should have an ardent zeal for the spiritual welfare and progress of souls and of her Community—showing great patience and forbearance with the weakness and imperfections of her Sisters. Let her be *prudent as the serpent,* not to permit herself to be surprised or deceived; and, on the other hand, as *simple as the dove*, never deceiving, but acting at all times with sincerity, avoiding all duplicity. She should be foreseeing and provident in all cases, never lightly harboring in her mind any diffidence or suspicion on slight grounds and without sufficient evidence. Finally, she should be united to God by the spirit of prayer, and assiduous in the care of the House, through a sense of duty—avoiding the dissipation to which the requirements of her office may expose her, by means of the spirit of prayer, and, on the other hand, a too great abstraction by the consideration of her responsibilities. The Holy Spirit will teach her these things more particularly in practice.

The authority of the Superioress should give her supernatural strength and efficiency in her administration, to prevent any relaxation in the observances of the Community, or in anything essential to Religious discipline and regularity, or in the rules of Religious modesty and propriety. Her aim should be to correct vice, to remove scandal and bad example, and, as much as possible, to banish all kinds of sin from the House of God; but let charity impart gentleness to her manner of action, and let the demands of authority be moderated and made agreeable by this sweetness of charity. The Superioress should remember that she has no authority for its own sake, but only to exercise that charity which must ever be the first motive that impels her to the exercise of her authority, as it is its end and its resting place; that is to say, she must use her authority only through motives of charity and to do good to others. Hence, we infer that her office obliges her at the same time to a life of repose and of activity; her repose must consist in charity, and her activity must display itself in the exercise of her authority under the impulse of charity. Hence, in all her actions, let her have, as it were, two objects in view, namely, authority, which she may readily cast off and relinquish, and charity, to which she must ever tend, and in which she must abide; thus passing gently from one to the other, she will never exercise her authority except at the expense of suffering to herself, and for the sake of charity towards others.

In accordance with this principle, let the Superioress act, not as a Lady and Mistress, but as the Mother and servant of all, treating her good and dear Sisters with mildness and affability, and granting them full liberty to call on her with perfect confidence, in all their necessities. Let her solicit, rather than command; invite and exhort, rather than compel or threaten. Let the Sisters, on their part, respond to this gentleness, by rendering an exact, willing and prompt submission, obeying the least sign, and even the intentions of the Superioress. Not, as the Apostle warns us, with vexation, or through necessity, for "*God loveth a cheerful giver.*" Nevertheless, this same Charity obliges the Superioress to act with severity and authority in case (which may God forbid!) she has to deal with obstinate and refractory characters.

The obligations of a Superioress are three-fold: those in regard to God; those which concern her neighbor, and those towards herself. (1) In regard to God her conduct should be marked with humble submission; adoring His Divine Majesty and acknowledging her own weakness and littleness, yet relying with confidence on the strength of Him who has said: "*Without me you can do nothing.*" (2) She should be respectfully submissive to the counsels and secret guidance of God, in the souls committed to her care. (3) Let her make frequent aspirations to God, the Father of light and grace—never undertaking anything of importance without having earnestly recommended it to God in prayer; considering herself only as an instrument, but as God's instrument, to accomplish works that have reference to Eternity. Finally, let her have recourse to prayer in all the spiritual and temporal necessities of the Monastery, daily recommending to God everything and every person under her charge.

In regard to her neighbor, let the Superioress exercise charity, patience, benignity, solicitude and edification—often recalling these beautiful words of the Apostle: "*Charity is patient, is kind; it seeketh not its own interests, but those of Jesus Christ; it suffereth all things, hopeth for all things and endureth all.*" Let the superioress spread everywhere—not the odor of sin and death, but that of Jesus Christ. In other words, let her be the good odor of Jesus in all her words and actions, as the Apostle teaches, " *We are the good odor of Jesus Christ.*"

As to herself, the Superioress should possess a spirit of disengagement from all earthly things, combined with an attraction for those that are heavenly, and great patience with others. Let her consider her charge as a cross which she must carry with submission to the movements of grace, and without any regard to natural taste or personal satisfaction. Let her make it a rule to herself and to others to follow the teaching of the Apostles: " *If we live in the Spirit let us walk in the Spirit,*" trying never to indulge habits, actions or inclinations that are purely natural, but to be always guided by the vivifying and sanctifying Spirit of the Son of God, our Lord, Jesus Christ.

It is strongly advisable for the Superioress to make, besides her ordinary examination of conscience, a particular one on the duties of her office and on the faults she may have committed in their discharge, with a view to correct, retrench or supply whatever she may discover, by the light of God, to be defective, and thus renew herself in the interior Spirit.

For this end the Superioress should, (1), profoundly adore the Holy Providence of God, which extends to all things, even the smallest, prescribing them with authority, and regulating them with sweetness. Let her endeavor to imitate this unwearied vigilance—this vigor and benignity—in all the requirements of her charge. (2) She should humbly venerate the Sacred Mystery of the Incarnation, in which God deigned to unite Himself, not only to the Spirit, but also to the body and flesh of man according to these words of St. John. *"And the Word was made Flesh."* He embraced the lowest things and those apparently least useful and honorable, wishing to sanctify and deify all by the plenitude of His Divinity. In like manner let the Superioress make it her disposition and chief study to devote herself humbly and charitably to all, and to diffuse throughout the Monastery the spirit of true sanctity. (3),

She should honor and imitate the Spirit of Christ in the government of His Church, and every part thereof, together with the souls specially consecrated to Him. Let her revere His presence, His power and His secret operations in all, not only rendering herself susceptible of the impressions of this Divine Spirit, but serving as His instrument to operate in the souls of others. In other words, let her be, not only a vessel to receive the grace of God, but also a channel whence this grace may flow into the souls committed to her care.

CHAPTER IV.

The Assistant.

When the Superioress is absent, the Assistant shall take her rank and place, and preside at all the assemblies in the Choir, Chapter-room, Refectory, Work-room,—in a word, at all the exercises of the Community. When the Rev. Mother is present, the Assistant shall hold the first rank after her, without any regard to seniority.

When the Superioress is disabled by sickness, or absent for her spiritual Retreat, or any other legitimate cause, the Assistant, by the fact, becomes responsible for the Community, and has the same authority as the Superioress, who may appoint another Sister as her aid;—but in this case, the latter is not to change her rank. The Assistant shall subsequently report to the Superioress all that may have transpired during the latter's absence. She should be to the Rev. Mother as an eye, a tongue, and a hand, to know and to see together with her, all that happens in the House; as also to make known her orders and to have them executed. Wherefore, let her be closely united in God with the Superioress, whom she should consider as the interpreter of His divine will. Let her greatly respect, and cordially assist her as her mother, endeavoring by all means, to inspire others with similar sentiments of reverence and affection. On the other hand, let the Superioress respect and support her Assistant's authority in regard to the other Sisters, never publicly disapproving her orders or censuring her conduct,—rather giving her all necessary directions in private, and thus guiding her, as much as possible, in her exterior as well as interior conduct.

The Assistant should be distinguished for regularity, assisting as punctually as possible at all the observances of the Community. Let her claim no distinction; be kind and affable towards the Sisters as the second Mother of the House; inspiring them with confidence, that she may serve as mediatrix in their behalf and relieve them in their necessities, as far as the duties of her office may permit. The Rev. Mother may sometimes charge her with the direction of such among the Sisters, as may wish to address themselves to her for their spiritual wants. Like the Superioress, the Assistant shall be called *Mother*, and all should revere her as such. But, while the office of the Superioress implies and involves authority, obliging her to act with power and energy; that of the Assistant supposes more love and condescension; hence, let the latter always entreat, rather than command.

The Assistant is the Rev. Mother's Counsellor by right, and has a decisive voice in

Council, as has been heretofore mentioned, Chapter VII, Part II, treating of the temporal Administration. She has, however, no right to make innovations, to change anything in the orders of the Superioress, or to act contrary to the latter's will, even during her absence. She is to give the Rev. Mother an account of the Community—informing her of the faults that may have been committed, and proposing the means she thinks proper to remedy the evil.

The Assistant should see every evening, that the Dormitory is closed at the hour prescribed, and that silence is observed. Let her also visit the cells, to see that all the Sisters have retired at the appointed time.

INSTRUCTION.

God, who is an infinite Agent, and who can do all things by Himself, wishes, nevertheless, to make use of secondary causes for natural effects, and to associate with Himself subordinate agents, to coöperate with Him in the works of grace: Not, indeed, through necessity, but in accordance with the economy established by His infinite Wisdom. In like manner as in the body, the head does not act by itself, but by means of the other members and faculties over which it presides, so should the Superioress, in honor and imitation of this divine economy, and by the order of God, as well as through a sense of her own incapacity, associate with herself aids and coöperators in the various functions of the Community. The Assistant ranks first among these, being, as it were, a link between the body and the head—receiving light and guidance from the Superioress, to impart them, in her turn, to the Community.

The instructions that have been given for the Superioress, may proportionately be applied to the Assistant, who should be one with her. Sharing the Rev. Mother's authority and responsibilty, she should be animated by the same spirit, have but one heart, and with due submission and dependence, adopt the same sentiments with the Superioress.

To fulfil her duties properly, the Assistant should be: (1) Humble, always cherishing sentiments of self-annihilation under the powerful Hand of God, and adoring His supreme dominion over all things. (2) She must be obedient, honoring the perfect submission of the angelic spirits to the least indications of the divine Will. Let her often invoke the Guardian Angels of the Monastery, and those of the souls under her charge, or with whom she may have any intercourse. (3) Let her be charitable and devout, frequently offering and uniting herself to the deified soul of Jesus, revereing His adorable Will and designs in regard to each soul in the Community, and drawing from his Sacred Heart, as from a glowing furnace, that zeal and ardent Charity with which she herself ought to be animated, and with which she must endeavor to inflame the hearts of others.

CHAPTER V.

The Treasurer.

The Treasurer is charged with all the property of the Community—all the funds, income, houses, farms, vineyards, lands, debts—in a word, with all business matters, and she is to answer the call of such as come to treat of these affairs—always, however, in accordance with the instructions of the Superioress and her Council; hence, let her be careful to keep everything in order. It is also the duty of the Treasurer to give leases, to improve and cultivate the ground, &c., to collect the amounts due for rent or on bills, never letting them accumulate. She should, however, never give a lease, or sign a contract without the approbation of the Superioress and her Council. Let her take care of all the business-papers of the Monastery.

The Sister chosen for this office should be judicious, prudent, trustworthy, cautious and zealous for the welfare of the Community, and have some experience in business matters, so that all may be able to rely on her management. She shall have a key to the Archives wherein are kept the original Title deeds, the Bulls and Briefs of our Holy Father, and other important documents—such as the Original Copy of the approved Constitutions, the Record of the Sisters' Profession, the Doll dressed to serve as a model for the Religious Costume, &c. She must also have one of the keys of the safe wherein is deposited the surplus money. On entering Office, she shall be shown the closed accounts of her predecessor, the Cash on hand shall be counted in her presence, and she must register all the gross provisions and the financial state of the Monastery.

The Treasurer should have a copy of the Title deeds and of the more important and perpetual contracts; or, she may engage a notary public to copy and sign them in a large book, which she must keep for reference in cases of necessity. The object of this precaution is not only that she may be well informed as to the state of affairs, but also to shun the risk of losing the original documents. Those to whom she may confide these documents must give her an acknowledgment of the same in presence of the Superioress and the Assistant, but she may give the copies of her own accord, noting, however, to whom, when and for what purpose they were given. When called to give notable receipts, she should have them signed by the Superioress, or, in her absence, by the Assistant.

The Treasurer shall receive all the money, whatever may be its source, and all the funds of the House should pass through her hands. She is to furnish or buy all the necessary provisions of flour, wine, oil, wood, &c., and give to the Housekeeper what may be required for the ordinary expenses. The Treasurer shall also receive the money that is drawn, according to necessity, from the safe with three locks, distributing it to the Housekeeper, who is responsible for the money and for the provisions entrusted to her, and of which she must subsequently give an account.

The Treasurer should have a large book, in which she shall register the Christian and family name, the parentage, country, and the date of each Sister's Entrance,

Vesture, and Religious Profession, together with the amount each has brought with her, the agreements made in regard to each one's dowry or pension; the receipts for the payment of said dowry, and other similar items—so as to keep a record of all. If the Superioress thinks proper, she may give the Treasurer an Assistant, to help her in drawing up her accounts, and in other business matters. The Sister thus appointed shall be carefully instructed by the Treasurer in all that concerns the affairs of the Community, as far as her talents and capacity may allow.

The Treasurer shall present her accounts to the Council every three months.

INSTRUCTION.

If we were pure spirits, like the Angels, we would be freed from the care of exterior things, and the grace and love of God would be the only treasures each soul would be required to preserve and increase. But, as our soul is confined within a mortal body, that weighs down and debases our mind which is capable of the sublimest aspirations—it is necessary, in order to keep it free and disengaged, that there be one charged to labor for the tranquillity of the others, and to take care of all the temporalities and the funds of the House, in order to apply them to the wants of her Sisters—the poor servants of Jesus Christ.

As this office must serve to spread the good odor and edification of virtue beyond the enclosure of the Monastery, the Sister who discharges its duties should, above all others, study to be, and to spread around her, the good odor of Jesus Christ, showing herself gentle, affable, patient and condescending towards all with whom she may have any business or intercourse. To this end, let her be more occupied with God than with herself, and thus, our Lord possessing and filling her interior faculties, will Himself spread the perfume of her virtue in her exterior relations with others.

Let her not, however, under pretext of recollection and devotion, become abstracted, careless or negligent in regard of the affairs of the House, for these, being her present obligation, demand due thought and attention, and thus she will find, even in temporal concerns, a treasure of grace and blessings for her soul; while our Lord, drawing her to Himself, will personally direct her in the requirements of her charge.

When pressed by a multiplicity of affairs, let her guard against excessive activity and eagerness, and against all impatient or angry emotions, gestures, or words in discussions — showing herself peaceful, calm, and hopeful in her difficulties, daily practising patience, humility, charity, and frequent recollection at the beginning, at the end, and during the intervals of her various duties.

The Treasurer should honor the holy souls who have glorified God in similar occupations, and who are now in Heaven, having attained sanctity by means of these very duties. Let her ask a share in their graces and virtues.

She should, by her duties and occupations, honor the exterior and interior duties and occupations of the Blessed Virgin as the Guardian of Jesus during His mortal life.

Lastly, the Treasurer should adore our Blessed Lord, ruling and directing by the power and gentleness of His Spirit, the exterior economy of His Church—and, as her work is for Him, let her labor with Him—having Him even more present to her mind than the action itself.

CHAPTER VI.

The Counsellors.

The Council of the Superioress is composed of the Assistant, the Treasurer, and two Counsellors elected by the Chapter. A new one should be elected each year, during the Octave of St. Ursula's; but all must never be changed at the same time, in order that there may be always some, acquainted with the state of affairs. In case of a Counsellor's absence, sickness, or other impediments, the Mother Superioress may substitute others in her place. The Sisters chosen to fill this office must be persons of acknowledge good sense and judgment, and possess experience or aptitude in business-matters.

Let the Mother Superioress always preside in Council; in her absence, this right devolves on the Assistant.

The Council should be convoked for all business-transactions,—for instance, to give leases, make contracts, deliberate on the construction of new buildings, to hear the Treasurer's and Housekeeper's accounts, and to consult on the admission of young ladies, as Postulants. In temporal matters, the Counsellors have a decisive voice, except when there is an equal number on both sides, in which case, the decision of the Superioress carries the point. But in matters of government, they have only a consultative voice, submitting to the judgment of the Superioress, whom they shall leave free to take whatever resolutions she thinks proper,—without disputing, murmuring, or complaining of the decision in question.

That one, among the Counsellors, who writes best, shall be appointed Secretary of the Councils and the Chapters held for business-transactions. She is to copy the resolutions that have been taken, neatly, accurately, and as dictated to her by the one who presides. These resolutions having been signed by both, let nothing more be added.

The Counsellors are under a very special obligation to promote the welfare of the Community, to warn the Superioress either in private, or when assembled in Council, of the faults that are committed, and of whatever they consider opposed to the Spirit of God, or prejudicial to the interests of the Monastery. Let them observe strict secrecy in regard to all that transpires at Council, remembering what has been said on this head in the Chapter on business-transactions.

INSTRUCTION.

Our divine Lord has said: "*Where there are two or three gathered together in my Name, there am I in the midst of them.*" (Matth XVIII, 20). Let Him therefore be regarded, honored, and invoked as present and presiding in Council where the Sisters are assembled in His Name and in the presence of His Spirit.

The Counsellors should especially honor the holy Apostles Peter, James, and John,—who were selected by our blessed Saviour to be His faithful companions in His most secret mysteries. Let them honor the zeal and ardent love of the first, the lively faith and confidence of the second, and the simplicity and purity of intention which distinguished the third.

CHAPTER VII.

The Mistress of Novices.

The Mistress of Novices should possess all general qualifications, if possible, in an eminent degree. She should be distinguished in the spirit and grace of her vocation, with which she ought to be thoroughly imbued, in order to communicate the same to her daughters; she should be regular and exact in the observance of all the Rules, in order to teach her Novices, not only by word, but also by example, and to conduct them as it were by the hand—directing them by interior and exterior means, and step by step in the path of Religious Perfection. Hence, let her be as assiduous as possible in discharging her duties of the Novitiate and always remain with her daughters during both their ordinary and their extraordinary recreations, to see that their deportment be always religious. Let her also accompany those who are called to the Parlor, and never leave them to converse alone with any person except their parents, and by the permission of the Superioress.

The Mistress may impose on the Novices whatever penances and mortifications she thinks proper—always acting with great prudence and discretion in this matter, as also in granting them ordinary liberties, permissions, and dispensations from the fasts of the Rule. Her principal care should be to inculcate the exact observance of all the Rules, Customs, and Regulations of the House, and to exercise her Novices in the practice of the vows they are to make to God. Let her strive to awaken in them a holy desire of Poverty, and accustom them to be exact in Obedience, not only to their Superiors, but also to the Rule, omitting no point thereof except through necessity and with permission. It would be well at times for the sake of emulation and encouragement, to induce them to vie with one another in the practice of virtue.

The Mistress should, once a week, see and speak to each of the Novices in private, concerning their trials and temptations, and the exterior employment of their time. Nevertheless, let her receive them and listen with gentleness, charity, and patience as often as they may wish to address themselves to her, showing them perfect confidence, but endeavoring to retrench all childishness, frivolities, extravagance, imperfections, and, as far as possible, all disquietude and scruples, which are frequently the ruin of young souls. Hence, let her draw them from this labyrinth, to make them walk in a free and wide path, full of confidence and noble aspirations towards God. To this effect, let her teach them to examine their conscience briefly, not only in their daily examinations, but also in preparing for Confession; exhorting them to apply themselves to the requisite interior sentiments, rather than to an over-exact research of their faults, and to make their Confessions with candor, simplicity, humility, and conciseness.

In giving spiritual instructions and conferences, let her accomodate herself to their capacity and disposition, and raise them little by little to the spirit of their vocation and in the grace of the Religious life. She should make them study the Catechism and all that regards the worship and service of God, including the exercises of Christian and Religious piety; namely, how to meditate properly, how to say the divine office, and perfectly to observe all its ceremonies, which latter, the Mistress should have rehearsed occasionally by the Directress of the Choir. She should also instruct the Novices in all the Religious Ceremonies, in the practices and observances of the Community, and in the Rules and Constitutions, which she must explain to them, inculcating great respect and esteem for every point thereof. Unless the Mother Superioress ordain otherwise, the Mistress should see all the letters which the Novices write or receive.

Let her, at least once a month, give the Superioress an account of what transpires in the Novitiate, and, once a year, about three months before the Novices' Profession, she should inform the Superioress' Council of their dispositions in general. This should be done with all possible sincerity, in order that, after having been questioned and examined by the Council, said Novices may be proposed to the votes of the Chapter, which decide whether or not, they are to be admitted. The Mistress should accustom her Novices to receive and listen to the Superioress with great respect whenever the latter visits the Novitiate; to give her a faithful account of themselves, and to have perfect confidence in her—reminding them that they are free to speak to the Rev. Mother in private, whenever such is their desire.

INSTRUCTION.

The Treasurer is the guardian of the temporal possessions of the Community, but the Mistress of Novices is the depositary of the most precious treasures in Religion, namely, the spirit and grace of our Vocation — fervor and regularity in the observance of the Rules and Constitutions. As the whole course of the Religious life depends, as a general rule, on the first impressions received in the Novitiate, and as the proper training of Novices is so important for the preservation and welfare of the Order, there is nothing to which the Superioress should give more consideration or which she should more earnestly recommend to God, than the choice of a wise, virtuous and devout Sister, to cultivate these young plants, and to be a source of grace and piety — not only to the Novices, but to the whole Community and for future times.

Let the Mistress of Novices consider, above all things, that the charge imposed on her surpasses her natural strength — that it implies the directing of a soul towards a supernatural end—the coöperation in the effects of her eternal predestination; she is to prepare a future Spouse for the Son of God and to labor for the establishment of His Spirit and Kingdom within her. Esteeming herself unworthy of so noble a ministry, let her implore light and unction from the Holy Spirit. Let her frequently recommend to God the souls under her charge, and become a true child of prayer to which she should devote herself as much as her time will allow, having recourse to it in all the necessities and trials of her office. She should constantly exemplify in her person, and teach her Novices to observe this saying of the Apostle: "*If we live in the Spirit, let us also walk in the Spirit.*" For, as life precedes action, she must implore this life of the Spirit, in order to act, speak, and direct these young souls —not according to her own sentiments, much less with violence and caprice, but by the principles and attractions of grace. Thus, little by little, and in proportion to each one's capacity, she will impress her Novices with motives of piety and the love of God—enabling them to perform all their actions "*in the Spirit,*" even as they should "*live* in *the Spirit.*" Let her, above all things, endeavor to make them recall and thus reanimate in themselves the pure object and intention which they had in view, on leaving the world and entering the Cloister; or rather, the design God had on them in calling them hither.

In imitation of St. Bernard, who, during his Noviceship repeatedly said to himself: " Bernard, Bernard, why hast thou come hither?" they should daily and frequently make use of these same words, to renew and strengthen themselves in their first fervor, which they should never permit to be, in the least degree, diminished. Moreover, as in former times, the sacred fire was kept constantly burning in the holy Tabernacle, and was never allowed to be extinguished, so should the Mistress of Novices be particularly careful that the sacred fire of fervor be always kept aglow among her daughters, and that they encourage one another in the sacred duties of the Religious life. When she sees any one among them suffering, afflicted or tepid, let her, without delay, seek to find out the cause of this coldness, in order to apply a remedy—to support, to encourage, and to offer the needed assistance.

To this effect, let her be to her Novices *a Mother*, bringing them forth with much pain and labor, in the spirit of the Religious life; a *Nurse*, full of care and solicitude, to make them drink the milk of piety and knowledge of the requirements of their vocation; finally, a *Mistress*, training and instructing them with prudence and love in the practice of virtue and in the functions of Religion. Let her love the Novices with a tender, but strong affection, inculcating, not a soft, cowardly, and effeminate devotion, but one that is true and solid, based on the mortification of the senses and natural inclinations, on an unaffectedly sincere humility and submission of will, and on the abnegation of their own judgment. Hence, let them be constantly exercised in these three points.

The Mistress should make her Novices understand and appreciate the singular grace of their vocation, as one of the first and greatest effects of their eternal predestination, that they may, every day of their life, render most humble thanks to God our Lord, loving and cherishing their vocation above all other states and conditions in the world, as being most meet and appropriate for them, since it has been assigned them in the eternal councils of God. Let them not, however, esteem themselves or their Order higher than the other Orders in the Church; but let them preserve their vocation as a precious deposit— as though these words of the Apocalypse were addressed to each: "*Hold fast that which thou hast, that no man take thy crown*" (Apoc. iii., 11).

However, as in the spiritual life there is neither permanence nor repose, it does not suffice merely to preserve this grace, it must be increased and perfected by a faithful coöperation and by interior and exterior practices. This is a task which they must daily re-commence, saying with the Psalmist: "*I have said: Now I begin; and this change is an effect of the Right Hand of the Most High.*"

It would, however, avail the Novices but little to be bound and devoted to their vocation, both voluntarily and by vow, if they be not animated by the spirit and the interior dispositions which this vocation implies and by which it is necessarily accompanied. This would be to have a body without a soul—to bear the Cross without unction. Hence, one of the chief cares of the Mistress should be to instruct and exercise the Novices in what might be called the cardinal virtues of an Ursuline. The first is a special love of purity of mind and body, which shall serve as a seed of this same virtue in the young girls whom God sends to them for instruction; the second is humility and simplicity of mind; this is the guardian of Chastity, having for its aids the virtues of Meekness, Obedience and Modesty; the third is zeal to serve and benefit their neighbor, and, inasmuch as their condition may allow, to impress others with the love and fear of their Divine Spouse; The fourth is a tender love and devotion towards our Savior Jesus, especially His sacred Humanity and blessed Infancy, and towards His beloved Mother, the Immaculate Virgin Mary.

Finally, as the direction of souls is styled by one of the Doctors, *the Art of arts*, and as it is a work of grace which depends more on the light of God than on our own views, lights and exertions, it is necessary that the Father of souls, that is to say, God the Holy Ghost, be Himself the

Teacher of this science and the Director of this work. Hence, the Mistress of Novices should humbly have recourse to Him, acknowledging that this divine art of instructing souls and of directing them by interior ways, is based on humility and not on self-sufficiency; that it is a lesson, not of memory, but of prayer; a science, not of words, but of practice—not of reasoning, but of submission, not of speculation, but of love—the love of Jesus, who sacrificed Himself for the salvation of souls. In this humble conviction, combined with prayer and meditation, consists the main point of the art of spiritual direction, and these are the two great essentials for the proper discharge of the duties that devolve on the Mistress of Novices.

Furthermore, let her honor, (1) The Holy Spirit replenishing and directing the Sacred Humanity of Jesus, in which and by which He operated in a manner ineffably divine. (2) The most wise and gentle conduct of Jesus with His Apostles. (3) His sacred intercourse with them during three years, and the sublime virtues He manifested during this time— virtues which she must strive to imitate, namely, His humility and meekness, His charity and efficiency, His spirit of prayer and His frequent retreats on the Mountain. (4) Let her honor the designs, the secret councils and desires of the souls of Jesus and Mary in regard to those under her charge—in the execution of which she is to be chiefly instrumental. Hence, let her frequently examine and study these designs and pray for their accomplishment. Finally, let her recognize the relations of souls with the Blessed Trinity, the Sacred Humanity of Jesus, the most holy Virgin, the holy Angels, and the Blessed Patrons and Protectors of our Order—to the end that she may unite herself to them, and offer them the souls committed to her charge.

CHAPTER VIII.

The Portress or Turn-Sister.

This office is so important that it should be confided only to one of the oldest, most discreet and zealous members of the Community—one who can be safely trusted, not only because of her fidelity, but also on account of her prudence in the observance of the Rule of Cloister. Let her strictly observe all that is prescribed on this subject in Chap. I., Part II. The same Sister shall have charge of the Door and of the Turn; nevertheless, some others should be appointed to assist her. It is for her to keep, during the day, the keys of the grating-doors and of the Turns of the House, excepting those of the Church and Vestry; but, at night, she must bring all the keys to the Superioress and take them again in the morning. Let her endeavor to show herself mild, affable and devout with outsiders, remembering that in her communications with them she must give edification and spread the good odor of the

Community. Let her be quick, so that persons may not be kept waiting in the Entry or at the Turn.

The Portress should never open the door except with the permission of the Superioress or of the one appointed by the Rev. Mother. She must be careful not to allow more persons to enter than may be necessary for the object for which they have been admitted, and never remain standing before the door when open, so managing, that when obliged to open it, she may not be seen face to face by those outside. She should never deliver any message at the door, nor receive or give letters to any person. When there is only a word to be said, she may say it through the small grate in the door; otherwise, let her send the persons to the parlor or to the Turn. The Portress should see all that is sent out of the House, and keep a written account of essentials. She must never leave the keys in the door.

Let her faithfully observe all that is prescribed in regard to the grates and Turns, remembering that she is responsible before God for the faults that may be committed against this rule, through her negligence or connivance. Hence, she should, as rarely as possible, open the grates, the doors of the parlor, or the large gate, before daybreak or after dark; and, in cases of necessity, let her be careful to have a light both in and outside. She must call no one to the Parlor without first informing the Superioress; and if there be any who go without permission, or who frequently receive visits without an accompanying sister to listen to the conversation, the Portress shall inform the Rev. Mother of this fact. Should a sister be called during the hours of Meditation, Divine Office, or any of the regular Observances, let the Portress politely beg to be excused from calling her, unless it be for matters of importance, for persons of distinction or for strangers. Accordingly, let her warn the Turn-Sisters in the Entry not to allow visitors to ring during these hours. The Portress should never deliver any messages from seculars to the sisters, or from the Sisters to seculars, except by an order from the Superioress, or, when the Novices are concerned, from their Mistress.

INSTRUCTION.

Jesus, our Blessed Lord, is the Door, and according to His word, if we enter by Him into the sacred pasture-grounds of Religion, we shall find life and grace. But, says a holy Doctor, the Holy Ghost is the Keeper of this Door; it is He who gives us admission and who opens to Jesus the door of our hearts, placing Him in possession of our souls. The office of keeping the door and the Turn belongs, therefore, chiefly to the Holy Ghost,—the Portress being only His aid and delegate, to receive and admit whatever comes from, or is sent by Him, and to dismiss and discharge all that does not come from Him, or that may be displeasing to Him.

To acquit herself worthily of this office, let her remember, in opening and closing the gates and doors, to open her heart to the Holy Spirit and to close it against all worldly and exterior objects. Let her especially honor the Holy Virgin exclaiming, *"Behold the Handmaid of the Lord,"* by which she gave admittance to the Eternal

Word, into her virginal womb and into the world. Let her also honor our Immaculate Mother as the "Gate of Heaven," beseeching her to admit us now to the grace and love of her Divine Son and hereafter to the Kingdom of His glory.

Finally, let the Portress adore Jesus as the Gate and the Holy Ghost as the Porter, who gives us admittance through Jesus, and who opens the door of our hearts that our divine Lord may dwell and repose therein forever.

CHAPTER IX.

The Housekeeper.

The general duty of the Housekeeper is to defray all the minor expenses of the House for food, clothing, and the ordinary furniture and accommodations of the rooms, as also, to take care of all the movable property of the Community. If the same Sister does not fill both offices, the Housekeeper should, from time to time, get money from the Treasurer for the ordinary expenses, and distribute it to the Turn-

Sisters, who are to make the necessary purchases, and who shall daily, or at least once a week give the Housekeeper an account of their commissions. She should have charge of the Lay and Turn-Sisters, and is to keep them employed in the various labors of the House. Let those, however, who have been assigned as aids to other Choir-Sisters, be under their special direction; for instance, the Sister who serves the Boarders shall be under the superintendence of the Directress of the Academy, and so of the others.

The Housekeeper has charge of all the provisions that shall have been left at her disposal by the Treasurer, whom she must inform in due time, when flour, oil, wine, wood, etc., are needed. It is for her to prescribe what the sisters Dispenser and Cook are to serve at table, and to see that the food is wholesome and properly prepared. Let her notice the wants of the Sisters, in order to provide for them in charity—but let her do nothing extraordinary without a command from the Superioress. She is to have the furniture of the House and kitchen repaired when necessary; hence, let her examine it from time to time, as also the cellar, the granary, and the bakery.

The Housekeeper should keep an Account-book, reserving one page for the statement of all the expenses, item per item, together with the date of the same; and on the opposite page, a similar statement of the receipts. These accounts shall be settled monthly in presence of the Superioress and the Assistant, and every three months in Council. On leaving her office, the Housekeeper shall give her successor an account of everything belonging to her charge, presenting a verified statement of the same, which shall be signed by both.

INSTRUCTION.

As we are composed of a body and soul, so, in all Communities, we may distinguish two elements, the one interior, the other exterior. Now, if the Superioress is the soul of the Monastery, the Housekeeper is its body, that is to say, she is to have the care of those exterior and temporal matters which constitute, as it were, the body of the Community. Hence, we may infer the great conformity and subordination that should exist between the Housekeeper and the Superioress. Let the former follow the latter's direction, submit to her influence, and be as it were, the living organ for the execution of her wishes, for on this admirable concord depend the perfect harmony and peace of the whole Community.

Let the Housekeeper carefully avoid extravagance, strive to economize the goods of the Monastery, and never make useless purchases. But, on the other hand, let her not manifest so great a desire of saving as to neglect the wants of the Sisters and of the Community in general. The first disposition implies the spirit of Poverty which she must love; the second, that of charity, in which she should abound. Let her be well grounded in the two great fundamentals mentioned by the Apostle: *"In the charity of God and in the patience of Jesus Christ."* Charity will make her endeavor to satisfy her Sisters in all that is reasonable and in her power; and, when compelled, through inability or other causes, to refuse them anything, it should be done with demonstrations of affection, and regret at not being able to accede to their request. Patience will help her to bear humbly and cheerfully, the little murmurs and complaints that may be brought against her and which she must endeavor to silence by her humility, never giving way to wounded feeling on their account. She should bear with confidence the poverty and scarcity that may be experienced in the Monastery, never treating herself better than the others, never reserving anything to herself, and never taking any new clothing for her private use, without the permission of the Superioress.

Let the Housekeeper adore God as Charity, imploring to be consumed in its divine flames. Let her especially honor the poverty and charity of the Son of God making Himself all to all, and conforming Himself to the requirments of our nature; and let her endeavor to imitate Him as far as her lowliness will allow, begging strength to endure all the trials of her charge. Let her revere the foréthought, solicitude and compassion manifested by the Son of God when, seeing the crowd that followed Him,

He exclaimed: "*I have compassion on this multitude,*" and forthwith He fed them in the solitude of the desert, thus proving the benign and efficient care of His Soul with regard to all in general and each in particular. Let her honor in Him the condition of servitude which He deigned to assume for the love of us, acknowledging herself to be the unworthy servant of His handmaids, recognizing Him in the person of each of her sisters, and hence, serving Him in them. Finally, let her refer and confide all to the holy Providence of God, as though she required no forethought, but, on the other hand, let her provide,—yet without anxiety and eagerness, as though she had nothing to expect from the Hand of God.

CHAPTER X.

The Directress of the Academy.

The Sister who holds this office is to have the general Supervision of all the Boarders, as also of their rooms and furniture, their health and instruction, their moral and religious training. Let her see that each

Teacher and Lay-Sister employed with them, does her duty, always keeping in view the instructions that have been given to this effect, in order to their exact observance.

Let the Directress or another, or, if necessary, two of the Sisters, be appointed to make their morning meditation in the Boarder's dormitory — that the children may never be left alone, and that they may be made to rise and dress modestly, at the appointed hour. If possible, the Directress should always preside at the Boarders' night and morning Prayer.

INSTRUCTION.

We should give nothing to others but what we have received from God. Hence, the Directress should be well grounded in solid virtue and divine love, in order to communicate the same to others. The *effusion* of the sacred waters of grace supposes the *infusion*; therefore, while the other offices serve to found and to confirm the Monastery and souls in their relations with God and themselves, those of the

Directress and the Teachers relate to the principal function of the Ursuline Order,—the training of young girls.

The chief object of devotion in these offices should be the most holy and amiable Infancy of Jesus, whom the Sisters should adore as a child in the innocent souls under their charge. Let them also honor the affectionate tenderness Jesus manifested for children, when He exclaimed: "*Suffer little children to come unto Me, for of such is the Kingdom of Heaven.*"

Finally, let them adore Jesus our Lord as a Master and the Doctor of Justice, for He Himself has said, "Your only Master is Jesus Christ."

It would seem, nevertheless, that the most appropriate mystery for Ursuline Schools is that of the Child Jesus at the age of twelve years in the midst of the Doctors in the Temple, interrogating them and answering their questions. While thus employed, He was found by His blessed Mother, and all wondered at His doctrine and His replies. This mystery is commemorated in the Gospel for the Sunday within the Octave of the Epiphany.

CHAPTER XI.

The Zelatrice.

This office should be entrusted to one of the elder members of the Community,—a Sister who is wise, zealous for the interests of the Community, and above all, very discreet; who, without being over anxious to sift matters, keeps, nevertheless, quietly vigilant to detect all that is done in the Monastery, contrary to the Rules, Constitutions, or morality. Let her notice if silence is observed, if all assist at the morning Meditation, at Divine Office, and at the regular Observances; if there are any disputes, &c., being vigilant, not only as to what concerns the Sisters individually, but also as to what is done in the different offices, and whatever regards the exterior requirements of the Community. She should mildly and in a spirit of Charity inform the Superioress of these matters; and the Sisters may address themselves to her whenever they perceive anything contrary to the Rule.

The Zelatrice should give her report in all simplicity to the Superioress, who may, if she thinks proper, call in the Assistant.

When the matter is of consequence, the Rev. Mother may communicate it to her Council, or even to the whole Chapter, so as to give a general admonition. This must, however, be done only after mature deliberation. Let the Zelatrice be careful not to divulge secret faults she may have discovered; she may, however, in charity, gently and prudently warn the Sisters against certain violations of the Rules and Constitutions. Let her carefully shun importunities, the spirit of criticism, and of exaggeration, and never insist too strongly on her own judgment. Having candidly expressed her views, let her humbly acquiesce in the decisions of the Rev. Mother, to whom is left the duty of correction. If, however, she sees in her a manifest connivance at the evil, she may consult the Father Director and submissively follow his counsel.

Let the Mother Superioress choose either the Zelatrice or any other Sister she thinks proper, to warn her in a spirit of charity and humility, not only of her personal defects but also of the faults she may commit in the exercise of her charge.

INSTRUCTION.

Our divine Lord exhorts us to watch and to keep ourselves always prepared, for we *know not the day nor the hour when He will come.* Let us not resemble the foolish virgins who slept and neglected to keep their lamps trimmed for the coming of the Bridegroom. It is expedient, therefore, that there be one appointed to watch, in order to ensure the greater peace and security of the others.

The Sister chosen for this duty should act with great charity, prudence and respect. Let her adore the knowledge and Omnipresence of God who sees all, penetrates all, who is everywhere and who searches the heart. Let her honor Jesus watching over us and praying to God His Father on the Mountain; let her unite herself to the angels and saints who love God uninterruptedly, even while we sleep; finally, let her humble herself frequently, and charge herself with all the faults of the Sisterhood, doing some penance for them and offering herself to God as a victim for the whole Community.

CHAPTER XII.

The Sacristan.

Let there be an inventory of all the gold and silver articles belonging to the Church, the original of which shall be kept in the Archives, while a copy of the same, verified and signed by the Superioress or her Assistant, shall be carefully preserved by the Sacristan. All that is required in the Church for daily use, or for Sundays and ordinary festivals, should be left to the care of the Sacristan; but the silver, the costly ornaments, and other valuable articles should be kept in a very secure place under a lock with two keys, one of which shall be kept by the Superioress and the other by the Sacristan. Let the same caution be observed with regard to the principal relics. When anything new is made or bought for the Church, the Sacristan must note it in her inventory, and on the first favorable opportunity, the same should be recorded in that of the Archives, together with the name of the donor.

Let the Sacristan pay special attention to cleanliness, neatness, and propriety in the vestments, the linen and other things beloning to her office. Let her see that the Lamp is always kept burning before the Blessed Sacrament, and take care of all the lamps and candles in the Church. Let her have the Altar always properly dressed, give the Vestments as required, noticing the color as indicated in the Ordo, and fold them carefully before putting them away. She should keep the Choir as well as the exterior and interior Sacristy very clean and prepare the seats when there is to be a sermon. Let her have Holy Water blessed every Sunday before Mass, so as to keep the Founts in the Church, as well as those in the cells and the different departments of the Monastery, well supplied.

The Sacristan should remind the Sisters, to prepare for Confession on the appointed days, and make a list of the Community, so that all may go in order. Let her ring a little bell, to assemble them, that the Confessor may not be obliged to wait; it is for her to call the Confessor when a Sister wishes to go to Confession at an unusual time; to remind the Superioress to engage an Orator for the solemn festivals, and for Lent and Advent. On such occasions, let her be careful to prepare the seat and to give out a surplice and baretta.

The Sacristan is to take charge of the keys for the grates in the Church, the Sacristy, and the Confessional, which she must open when necessary, and close at the end of the Exercise. At the time of Communion, let her get the key of the Communion-grate from the Superioress, to whom she must return it immediately after Mass. Let neither the Sacristan nor others be permitted to stand before the grate in the Vestry, to speak to the Confessor or to the acolyte, much less to strangers, unless it be in passing, or in cases of necessity and with the express permission of the Superioress; nor is it allowed to receive any note, letter, message, or other things, except with the same permission and consent. The Sacristan should have the Church-door opened and closed at specified times; at night, she is to close all the windows in the Choir and Vestry, and carry the keys of the Church to the Rev. Mother's cell. On leaving her office, let her give her successor the inventory of all the things in her employment, together with the directory of her charge.

INSTRUCTION.

If all, even the least, offices in Religion are pleasing to God, when performed in a spirit of charity, how much more so must be that which is exercised directly in His service—namely, the decoration of the Church and the preparing of the requisites to celebrate the stupendous mystery of our Salvation! Hence, the Sacristan should devote herself to her duties with special reverence and piety, begging the grace and ingenuity to acquit herself thereof in a worthy manner.

Let her consider herself the guardian of the Chapel, of the Blessed Sacrament, and all that relates to it; applying her whole mind and placing her chief delight in striving to handle holy and consecrated things in a spirit of sanctity, reverence and devotion.

To perform her office worthily, let the Sacristan honor: (1.) The most holy and Immaculate Virgin Mary, who was interiorly as well as exteriorly occupied with her little Jesus in the stable of Bethlehem, and during the whole of His Infancy—contemplating and adoring Him in spirit, loving Him with all her heart, nourishing Him at her virginal breasts, working for Him with her pure hands, and rendering Him all the services of a Mother, a Nurse, and a Handmaid, always with the most perfect and exalted dispositions. (2.) Let her honor St. Joseph, who was so humble and devoted in his service of Jesus and Mary, supporting them by the labor of his hands. (3.) Let her emulate the reverential homage of the holy Angels, who ministered to the Infant Jesus, and who still minister to Him in His adorable Sacrament, full of awe and love. Thus shall the Sacristan be associated in her office with the holy Angels, with St. Joseph, and with our Immaculate Mother.

CHAPTER XIII.

The Directress of the Choir.

As it is the duty of the Directress of the Choir to regulate and direct the Divine Office, she should attend this holy Exercise with exactitude. Nevertheless, let the Superioress appoint an assistant to supply the place of the Directress, in case of absence, in order that one or the other may be present at each Office. The Directress should have a Calendar or Directory of both the ordinary and the extraordinary feasts, together with a copy of the rubrics and ceremonies, which she must study and learn perfectly, so as to be able to instruct others. Let her be careful to notice that the Divine Office be said with precision and solemnity, as directed in the Ceremonial; and let her prudently correct the faults committed in Choir.

She should have a Tablet, on which she is to note, every Saturday, the order to be observed by those who are to officiate at the Divine Office, say the Verses, and other minor duties, such as reading and serving in the Refectory, etc. Before hanging up this Tablet, she shall present it to the Superioress for approval. She is also to indicate the Office that is to be said on Sundays and festivals. On extraordinary occasions, such as the Vesture, Religious Profession, or the Interment of a Sister, the Directress should remind the Community some time previous, and have a general rehearsal of the ceremonies.

On receiving the announcement of the death of a Sister belonging to one of the houses of the same Congregation, the Directress should hang up the notice in a convenient place, that the Community may be reminded of the Offices and prayers prescribed for the departed soul; and when it shall please God to call to Himself one of the members of the House, let her inform all the other Communities, and see that the customary prayers, Offices, and ceremonies are performed for the Deceased.

INSTRUCTION.

The Choir is the principal and most honored Department in the Monastery: it is a holy place, consecrated to the Holiness of God, and destined to sanctify our souls—a sacred place, in which we enter into communication and familiar intercourse with God, and He with us—it is a blessed spot which should be kept in view from all the other departments of the Monastery, even as Daniel contemplated the Temple from his cell in Babylon. Hence, the Sister who directs the holy Exercises performed therein should be animated by angelic sentiments, since she is occupied on earth with what the Angels do in Heaven, where they incessantly sing the praises of God. As all her treasure is in the Choir, here too should be her heart.

Let her study to render herself fit for this office, by learning to psalmody, to chant, and to entone properly; and familiarize herself with the rules and directions for all the Offices and ceremonies.

To perform her duties well and worthily, the Directress of the Choir should (1) be recollected in God, holding frequent conversations with the Angels and Saints, whose functions she must imitate—honoring the uninterrupted chants, benedictions, praise, honor and glory which they and all the Blessed offer to God throughout all ages, "both *day and night*," as the sacred Text expresses it. (2.) Let her unite herself to the Blessed Virgin, honoring her interior jubilation as expressed in her beautiful and sublime canticle, the "*Magnificat,*" as also while she bore the divine Infant in her chaste womb and dwelt in His presence on earth, particularly during His holy Childhood. Finally, let her raise herself even to the soul of Jesus, entering into His sentiments and sacred dispositions of reverence, adoration, and love, honoring the glory He continually gave God His Father, by His annihilation in our nature, as well as by His operations and divine elevations.

CHAPTER XIV.

The Infirmarian.

The Infimarian shall have the general care of all that regards the Infirmary and the service of the sick. Let her keep a memorandum of all the furniture, table-service and utensils that belong to her department, being careful to keep them separated from those of the Community. She should see that everything be in accordance with religious simplicity, but very clean and convenient. The rooms must be kept very neat and orderly; they may be decorated with framed pictures, evergreens, and flowers according to the season; even perfumes may be used when necessary. When the Infirmarian deems it expedient, she should obtain the Rev. Mother's consent to call in the Doctor or Surgeon, and either consult him at the grate, or, if necessary, conduct him into the enclosure, never conversing with him except on matters relating to the sick; and let her never detain him in the Infirmary longer than may be necessary. When there are many sick at one time, she should ask for some assistance; and in case it be necessary to sit up several nights in succession, she should see that this is done alternately, and that those who have watched by the sick afterwards get the needed rest and refreshment.

The Infirmarian should inform the Superioress as soon as she perceives that a Sister is seriously indisposed, in order to have her removed to the Infirmary where she is to provide for the patient's necessities and alleviation. Let the Infirmarian notice the beginning and the different stages of the disease, in order to give a correct report to the physician, whose prescriptions as to the diet, the quantity and quality of the food and remedies, and other necessaries, must be punctually obeyed. Hence, let her see that nothing is neglected, and never give anything that might prove injurious, under pretext of gratifying the patient. Let all the sick, including even the Superioress, be under the direction and superintendence of the Infirmarian, whom they shall obey with exactitude in all that regards their illness, alleviation and remedies; thus, while unable to act or to govern, they will learn, at least, to suffer and to obey.

The Infirmarian should inquire of the Superioress which Sisters should be allowed to visit the sick—being careful that nothing be said or done that might prove injurious to the patient. She may call some to entertain the sick; but let her dismiss them when she thinks proper.

When the disease is contagious, let the Infirmarian nurse the sick courageously, offering herself to God as a victim of charity. Nevertheless, for her own sake as well as that of others, she should use all reasonable precautions, allowing no one to enter the sick-room, except with the express permission of the Superioress; and let her keep apart all that is required for the use of the patient, to prevent the disease from spreading.

While attending to the wants of the body let the Infirmarian evince great zeal for the salvation of the soul. When she perceives that there is danger of death, let her give a timely warning, and see that the patient receives the last Sacraments in a state of consciousness. In case of a protracted illness, she should ask the Superioress what is to be done for the consolation of the sufferer.

When Holy Communion is brought to the sick, the Infirmarian should remind the Sisters to say the prayers specified for such occasions. Let her also take measures that there be a Priest to assist the sick in their last moments; at such times, whether it be during the day or night, she shall ring the bell, to assemble the Sisters around the death-bed. It is for the Infirmarian to prepare the body of the deceased, according to custom, for burial. The remains should, if possible, always be kept twenty-four hours.

INSTRUCTION.

If it be true that the measure of our love for God is to love Him without measure or limitation, we may give the same rule for the measure of the charity which the Sisters should exercise towards the sick; for in this there can be no excess, since our Lord not only assures us that He will consider as done to Himself whatever is done to the least of His, but He often deigns to assume the form of a poor sufferer, to give His servants at divers times and occasions the merit of practising heroic acts of mercy and charity towards the sick.

Let the Infirmarian frequently exercise herself in the virtues of patience and charity — patience, to support the ill-humor, vexations and whims into which the sick are often surprised by their sufferings and privations; and to bear the labor involved in their service, and the disagreeable odors of the sick-room — all with cheerfulness, and never betraying her annoyance or disgust. Her charity should manifest itself, not only in serving the sick with alacrity and, when possible, with condescension to their wishes, but also in relieving them by every means in their power — consoling them and diverting them by little innocent and devout contrivances. Let her always show herself gentle, serviceable, and equally kind to all, amusing them by some witty or enlivening narrations, or by some recreative reading; finally, let her show them implicit confidence, trying, nevertheless, by mild and adroit means, to make them practise holy resignation, patience, tranquility and obedience in their infirmities, and to divert themselves from their saddening impressions.

Besides these dispositions of patience, charity and humility—serving the sick in the lowest offices, disdaining nothing, yet neither overburdening herself lest she sink under the weight—the Infirmarian should, in order to acquit herself worthily of her charge, adore Jesus Crucified in each of her patients; for each bears the impress of some one of His sufferings, whereas He bore those of all. Therefore, let her serve them with as much joy and alacrity as it it were our Lord in person.

Let her adore Him prostrate with His face on the ground in the Garden of Olives—enduring before God His Father all our weaknesses and sufferings; let her also have a special devotion to His sacred Wounds—to draw from them strength, love and a salutary unction against all kinds of afflictions.

She should have a special devotion to the most holy Virgin under her titles of "Health of the Sick," and " Refuge of Sinners"—frequently invoking her as such in behalf of the sick, for whose intention she should perform some devotions in her honor, especially when they are at the point of death. Let her beg for them the plenitude of all graces — the final accomplishment of God's wishes and designs on their souls, and the perfection of His love, which is to continue throughout eternity, such as it will have been at the moment of death.

Lastly, she should implore for them the grace to die, not only in the state, but in the very act of divine love.

When alone with a sick person in her agony, let the Infirmarian endeavor to console and encourage her, making with her frequent acts of contrition, self-oblation and love. She might repeat slowly and distinctly some invocations of the Litany of the Holy Name, or that of the Blessed Virgin, or else say the prayers for the agonizing.

CHAPTER XV.

The Minor Employments in the Monastery.

Let the *Sister in charge of the various apartments* take care of all the furniture, see that nothing is wanting in the rooms; that the furniture be examined and exchanged in due time, and that it be preserved and repaired in such a manner that nothing may be lost or spoilt through negligence; and that there be nothing in the rooms contrary to religious poverty and simplicity. Let her keep a list of all the furniture in the House, and take note of the new articles that may be made or purchased.

The Seamstress or Robiere shall have charge of all the Habits; let her mend the old and make the new, keeping all in order, and separating the good from those that are worn out. She is expressly forbidden to gratify any one by the least oddity, singularity or superfluity, observing exactly what is prescribed for the cut and make of the Habits. Let her take away the winter Habits after having distributed those for summer, and *vice versa*, being careful to pack them up properly. She must never leave to any Sister more than is absolutely required, and see that there be always some Habits for a change. The old ones should be properly mended as long as they will serve in accordance with religious poverty. The *Robiere* must never give a new Habit without the permission of the Superioress. Let her give the Housekeeper an account of the material she has received from her, informing her of the use she has made of it; let her also give the Housekeeper a memorandum of the cloth and other necessaries required in her employment. The Superioress shall give her aids when she deems it expedient.

The Lingere shall take care of all the linen in the House; let her keep it neat and orderly as belonging to our Lord Jesus and destined for the use of His spouses. She is to mend and distribute it, not only in the cells for the requirements of the Sisters, but also in the Refectory, Storeroom and Kitchen; and take it up when soiled, to have it washed and folded. All the linen should be marked and counted, so as to be easily distributed. Let the Lingère keep a memorandum of all the linen she receives, in order to give an account of it at the end of the year; and let her be careful to inform the Superioress when anything is missing. No one should keep any linen in particular, but in case of accidental necessities or requirements, let the Lingère supply the Sisters with charity. The Sisters' linen must never be starched, this being allowed only for that of the Church, which is under the Sacristan's care. Let the Lingère combine neatness and cleanliness with religious simplicity, being careful to guard against the introduction of vanities or singularities.

The Sister Dispenser shall distribute the bread, wine, salt, oil and butter; in a word, all that is required for the meals. Let her give breakfast, according to the custom of the country, to such of the Sisters as may need it, and in special cases of necessity let her follow the directions of the Mother Superioress. Everything should be kept locked in the storeroom, which she must keep very clean. Let the Dispenser see that nothing is wanting, and also that nothing be wasted, misspent or spoilt; hence, let her carefully put away all the bread and the other things that are left after meals. The food shall be distributed equally to all, except to the infirm, whose treatment is subject to the orders of the Superioress.

The Cellarer shall have charge of the wine and the cellar, which she should visit frequently, noticing if the casks are well bound. Let her use forethought, to give timely information when anything is wanting.

The Refectorian is charged with all that belongs to the Refectory, which she must be careful to keep very clean. She is to set the tables, and, after meals, to fold and put away the table-cloths, etc. If the Rev. Mother thinks proper, two or three of the aforementioned employments may be given to one Sister.

The Sister Gardener shall see that the garden is well kept, that the walks are clean and convenient for the Sisters' promenade. She should, with the permission of the Superioress, ask for laborers, to employ in due season, in ploughing the ground and in sowing and planting. Let her gather the fruit and vegetables, and try so to manage that the Community may reap the fruits of her industry and labor.

The Sister Cook.—All the Lay-Sisters should learn how to cook; nevertheless, let there be a principal one whom the others shall assist in turn, as they may be commanded. They are to be under the supervision of the Housekeeper, and must obey all she ordains for the treatment of the Sisters. Let no one, except the Sister Infirmarian, ever be allowed to cook or season anything in particular, without the Rev. Mother's express permission; even the Infirmarian shall be allowed this privilege only in favor of the sick.

The chief cook should be faithful in preparing all that has been prescribed for the meals, according to the orders she has received—observing the weight, quantity and quality of the food, as specified by the Housekeeper, who should give her a directory of what is to be prepared on different occasions—that is to say, on ordinary days, on days of abstinence, on fast days, and on solemn Feasts, on which latter the Community shall be served to some extras. The Cook should endeavor to season and prepare the food properly, through respect for the Community, making it her care and pleasure to treat the poor servants of Jesus in a becoming manner. Let her, however, always keep within the limits of Religious Poverty and simplicity—avoiding too great expense and all manner of extravagance, being as saving as possible, especially in the use of wood. Let her slice and serve the food equally, never gratifying one more than another, excepting the aged and the infirm; but even in regard to these she must follow the Housekeeper's directions. If there be any Sister who does not ordinarily partake of a certain dish, the Cook should take note of it and inform the Housekeeper. If this be only for a limited time, the latter may provide; but in case of habitual requirements, the Superioress must be consulted, and she will ordain what charity may demand.

Let the Cook be careful to collect all that is returned from the Refectory, and dish what is best for the second or the "Poor Table," or for the Turn-Sisters. She should have a list of all the kitchen utensils, which she must preserve and keep clean, being careful that nothing be spoilt or broken.

INSTRUCTION.

As there is nothing little in the House of God where all shall be weighed in the scales of the Sanctuary—that is to say, according to the measure of love with which it is accomplished, and not according to the quality of the action itself,—the Sisters should desire and more willingly embrace the minor employments and such as involve a state of dependence, rather than the more honorable offices, endeavoring to acquit themselves thereof in a spirit of humility and dependence in regard to the other Sisters and with charity and diligence; with all the more reason, as they are not required to command and govern, but to obey with exactitude, remembering that they are doing the work of God as well as the other Sisters. Let them honor especially the condition of servant which our Blessed Lord assumed, according to those words of the Apostle, "*taking the form of a servant,*" and these of truth and humility: "*The Son of Man came not to be ministered unto, but to minister; and he who would be the greatest among you, let him be the least.*"

The Sisters should adore Jesus prostrate at the feet of his Apostles and washing them, not excepting even those of the traitor Judas. Finally, they should desire to serve the Blessed Virgin in their quality of servants of her Son — honoring all the services she rendered Him during His sacred Infancy.

Let the *Seamstress* ask with the Prophet, to be clothed with the garment of salvation, or with the spirit of Jesus, our Redeemer, and let her practically verify in herself this beautiful exhortation of the Apostle: "*Put ye on the Lord Jesus.*"

The *Lingere* should honor and imitate the holy Virgin who, before laying her little Jesus in the manger, wrapped Him in the clean, white linen she had prepared; for she, too, has similar offices to perform for our Blessed Lady in the person of her Sisters, the servants of that Immaculate Queen.

Let the *Dispenser* be a St. Martha, occupied in honoring and serving her good Master, whom she should recognize, honor and serve in the person of His hand-maids; let her imitate this Saint and guard against too great eagerness.

The *Sister Gardener* should adore Jesus in the quality of Gardener which He deigned to assume when He appeared to His beloved St. Mary Magdalen. Let her beg Him to cultivate the soil of her heart, to uproot thence all noxious weeds, and to plant therein fruits of eternal life.

The *Sister Cook* should, at times, contemplate in her fire the eternal pains of the fire of hell; at other times, the strength and efficacy of divine love, which, like material flames, converts everything into itself. Let her also consider (1) the weakness and humiliation of this miserable life, which requires so many things for its sustenance; (2) the curse and punishment of sin, in our being condemned to eat our bread by the sweat of our brow; and (3) the repose and felicity of Paradise, where there will be neither hunger nor thirst, but a perfect satiety in God. Finally, bearing in mind the words by which our Blessed Lord will address His elect on the Day of Judgment, "*Come ye Blessed of my Father, for I was hungry and ye gave me to eat;*" let her frequently beg to merit a share in this blessing, by her fidelity in serving her Sisters.

CHAPTER XVI.

Dispositions for all the Employments of the Lay-Sisters.

In order to perform their duties with humility, exactitude and devotedness, let the Lay-Sisters honor and imitate (1) the most holy and devout services which our Blessed Lady rendered Jesus during His amiable Infancy, clothing and nourishing Him with the most exalted dispositions and sentiments of love and reverence; (2) the humble services and obedience which Jesus, in His Youth, rendered to Mary and Joseph, as implied in these words: *"He was subject to them;"* (3) the services which the Angels of Heaven rendered Jesus, their Sovereign King, while on earth, both during His Infancy and in His later years, according to the sacred Text: *"Angels ministered unto Him;"* (4) the devotedness, activity and eagerness with which St. Martha welcomed, served and treated her divine Guest and honored Master. Lastly, the two principal dispositions of the soul of Jesus in all His actions and sufferings, namely: His obedience to His Father and His love for souls.

Let the Sisters endeavor to imitate these, performing all their actions and labors through motives of love and obedience, and let them bear in mind this counsel of St. Paul: "*Whether you eat or drink, or what else soever you may do, do all for the glory of God.*"

Let them daily renew their intention of thus referring all to the glory and love of God, accustoming themselves to raise their hearts to Him at the beginning, and frequently during the course of their work, by making the sign of the Cross, invoking the holy Name of Jesus and Mary, or making other short aspirations.

CHAPTER XVII.

The Obligation of the Sisters to Observe the Constitutions.

Although these Rules and Constitutions are not of themselves binding under pain of sin, except in what regards the essential vows; nevertheless, contempt of them, and wilful negligence in their observance would not be free from guilt; and this inobservance would deprive the soul of those manifold graces which God showers on such as serve Him faithfully. True, these Rules and Constitutions are not absolute Commandments of God, but they express His desires and His will in regard to those whom He has called to this Order. Hence, voluntary infractions of the same cannot but be culpable, because of the sinful circumstances which accompany such transgressions. How great would be the infidelity of one, who, having been called by the divine Spouse, would deliberately fail to meet His wishes and designs—disdain His graces, despise His caresses and make no effort whatsoever to merit His love! This is to be feared in Religious life where no fault is slight, and where one can hardly be saved in a state of mediocrity; for God Himself declares that he prefers a soul that is cold to one that is tepid—that is to say, persons in the world and given to its vanities, are less displeasing to Him than tepid and negligent Religious, who, having been delivered from the Sodom of the world, look back, and, like Lot's wife, become transformed into statues of salt— that is to say, they constantly desire what is no longer permitted them. They are of the world by an effect of their will, while they are Religious by the necessity of their vows.

Let the Sisters, therefore, lovingly embrace the Rules and Constitutions which God offers them. Let them observe the same with fidelity, and they may rest assured that, by this means, they will draw down on themselves an abundance of every grace and blessing.

INSTRUCTION.

We here give a summary and synopsis of the sentiments of piety and of the interior dispositions which should animate us in the observance of our Rules—not, indeed, with the intention of binding or limiting ourselves to those here suggested, but they may serve as a light to prepare our souls to receive the impressions of the Holy Spirit, to follow His guidance, to coöperate with His graces, and to render ourselves worthy of this exhortation of the Apostle: "*If we live in the Spirit, let us also walk in the*

Spirit!" That is to say, as our body lives by our soul, so should our soul live by the Spirit of Jesus; and as our mortal flesh is animated by our soul, so should our soul be animated by the Spirit of Jesus which sanctifies it. Our body lives by the soul a natural and human life; but our soul should live by the Spirit of Jesus a supernatural and divine life. Our body cannot live without being united to the soul; neither can our soul live unless it be united by grace and love to the Spirit of Jesus. Now, as we use material food and suitable refreshments to preserve our corporal life, so also, in order to sustain the life of the Spirit—that supernatural and divine life of our soul—we need a divine nourishment, namely: the Body and Blood of Jesus consubstantially united to His Divinity; and this He bestows on us, in order to make His Spirit live in ours. This, then, is the soul and life of our soul—our eternal life. It is by this means that we shall *live in the Spirit,* and so living, we shall *also walk in the Spirit.* That is to say, as our soul, which is the principle of our life, is likewise the principle of all our movements, functions and operations; so should the holy Spirit of Jesus, which vivifies and sanctifies us, cause us to act and be our attraction, our principle and our centre. It is a spirit of grace and love—a spirit of life and charity—that charity which should be our only motive in beginning, continuing and ending our actions, for it comprises all other holy dispositions.

Let this charity be the beginning, the middle and the end of our life, for it is an abridgement of the Christian Law and of the Rules and Constitutions framed for the Daughters of the Mother of grace "*and beautiful love,*" and of the glorious St. Augustin, that fervent Doctor of the Church and Patriarch of Religious, who tells us, "*Love God, and then do what you please.*" Yes, let us love God and Jesus Christ His Son, our divine Lord, for He commands us to love Him, and threatens with eternal torments those who do not love Him; but to those who keep this commandment He promises an eternal Crown. Let us love God, for He is Charity, and "*he that abideth in Charity, abideth in God.*" Let us begin on earth what we hope to continue in Heaven, where our life and only occupation will be an uninterrupted exercise and act of divine love; and where, if God will deign to show us mercy, we shall live and reign forever among the Blessed. Let us, therefore, never cease to love Him who is the consummation and the reward of those who love. He is Goodness itself — infinitely amiable, and the only One capable of loving Himself worthily — that is to say, infinitely. Yes, we shall love Him in the desirable Paradise of love, that Abode of glory; we shall love Him unalterably and uninterruptedly throughout an endless Eternity.

REMARKS ON THE INSTRUCTIONS.

The foregoing Instructions have been given us by Rev. Father Francis Bourgoing, Superior-General of the Oratory of Jesus, to teach us how to combine the spirit of grace and piety with the exterior observance of the Constitutions which his Reverence has drawn up for us; thus facilitating the cultivation of interior dispositions, amid our exterior occupations.

Let us, therefore, receive them as heaven-sent lights, whose bright rays are to guide our footsteps in the path of salvation and perfection. Let us hearken to them, as to so many divine exhortations, teaching us how to perform holy, religious, and perfect actions, in a holy, religious, and perfect manner. Let us cherish them as a treasury of inestimable value, whence we may draw the true riches of all Christian virtues. Let us not leave this treasure buried in the ground; rather, let us be careful to make daily, a holy and constant use of it, in order to satisfy the obligations of the holy state we have embraced, and thus render ourselves worthy Spouses of Jesus Christ.

CONCLUSION.

"We, Francis Bourgoing, Superior General of the Congregation of the Oratory of our Lord Jesus Christ, in consequence of the design formed some years since by the Sisters of the Congregation of St. Ursula, to embrace the Religious Life,

" under the title of "*The Presentation of
" the Blessed Virgin in the Temple,*" and un-
" der the Rule of St. Augustin, have, at
" their urgent, and frequently reiterated
" petition, drawn up for their use, the fore-
" going Constitutions. The special profes-
" sion which they make, of educating
" young girls in the spirit of piety and
" morality, induced us to add several in-
" structions suitable for this object—to
" those generally requisite for souls who
" embrace the Religious State. We have
" moreover, given them another little man-
" ual, containing diverse instructions and
" interior dispositions. It is divided into
" chapters corresponding to those of the
" Constitutions, that these may be prac-
" tised with the unction of grace and senti-
" ments of piety.* These being the soul
" and spirit of the Religious Life, we exhort
" the Sisters to make a holy and faithful
" use of them. Let them love their voca-
" tion as being most sacred; let them
" esteem their Institute, and exercise its
" functions with fervor, exactitude, and

---

*It has been deemed advisable to insert each Instruction immediately after its corresponding chapter of the Constitutions.— *The Translators.*

" piety, as they are destined to form Jesus
" Christ in themselves and in the young
" souls whom they are called to instruct.
" Finally, let them preserve inviolably, a
" holy union and charity among them-
" selves, and besides this general bond, let
" there be a constant uniformity among the
" Monasteries of the Order."

DIRECTORY,

Containing the Exercises, Customs and Practices, both exterior and interior, which the Ursuline Religious of the Presentation of our Blessed Lady should observe during the course of the day.

(1.) The Sisters shall rise at four o'clock in summer, from Easter until St. Michael's, and at half-past four in winter, from St. Michael's until Easter. Let them commence the day by an invocation of our Lord Jesus Christ, making the sign of the cross, and saying some short prayer to our Blessed Lady.

(2.) Let them take half an hour to dress themselves, attend to their necessities and make their beds; they must not leave their rooms before being entirely dressed.

(3.) During this time, they shall observe profound silence; go about without noise, and perform their actions quietly, remembering that they are soon to go to Meditation.

(4.) Let all assemble in the same place, for Meditation; listen attentively to the reading of the points, and devote one hour to this holy exercise, which begins at half-past four in summer, and at five o'clock in winter.

(5.) After Meditation, say together, Prime, Tierce, Sexte, and None, of the Blessed Virgin's Office, during which, as well as afterwards, they may recall the points that struck them most forcibly during Meditation, that these may serve as means of recollection during the whole day.

(6.) Let them employ the time between Office and the Holy Sacrifice of the Mass, in attending to particular necessities.

(7.) Assist at the Holy Sacrifice which, in summer, shall be offered a little after six, and in winter, about half-past six o'clock. After Mass, repair to an appointed place, where the Superioress, in the name of all, offers to God, the actions of the day. Hereupon, the Sisters may say the Morning-acts in private, and then go to the Refectory, to breakfast in silence. The time that remains from breakfast until ten o'clock, may be employed by each in attending to her particular wants—always preserving interior recollection, never speaking without necessity, and then, always in a low voice, which practice must be observed throughout the whole day, except during the hours of recreation.

(8.) At ten o'clock, repair to the Community-room, each having some work of her employment. Those who have to practise psalmody or singing, may do so during the first half hour. At half-past ten, the Sister named on the tablet that is hung at the door of the Community, shall begin the Spiritual Reading.

Sundays and Festivals should be spent in exercise of piety and devotion.

At eleven o'clock, the hour of retreat, let all repair to the Choir, to say together, the

Litany of the Blessed Virgin and make their Particular Examination during ten minutes; immediately after which, say the Beads, either in the Chapel or walking about, as each may desire. After the Beads, say the Litany of the Saints, with only the last Prayer, for the living and the dead. On Fridays, the Litany of the Holy Name of Jesus is said instead of that of the Saints. The time that remains before dinner may be employed in Spiritual Reading, prayer, or other particular necessities.

At noon, repair punctually to the Refectory for dinner. On Fast days, commanded by the Church, dine at eleven o'clock.

(9.) On Sundays and feasts of obligation, let the Sisters sing or say the Vespers of the day. On the Feast of Christmas and the three days of Tenebræ, they shall say the whole of the Grand Office, according to the Roman Breviary. On All Saints' day, let them say, besides the Office of the Blessed Virgin which is not interrupted on this feast, the Vespers, Matins with nine Lessons, and Lauds of the Dead, for All Souls' day. This same Office shall be said for a deceased of the House; for those of other Houses of the same Congregation, the Sisters shall psalmody in a low voice Vespers, Matins with three Lessons and Lauds.

(10.) The Lay-Sisters shall say every day ten *Paters* and *Aves* for Matins and Lauds; five for Prime, Tierce, Sexte, and None, and three for Vespers and Complin. For the Grand Office of the Dead and that of Christmas, they shall say thirty-three *Paters* and *Aves*, and a *Credo*, besides the Beads, which they must say every day.

All should observe silence and great modesty.

(11.) The Sisters shall always have about an hour and a half for Recreation after dinner; then go to the Choir for the *Sancta Maria*, after which they may attend to their employments, as directed in the 5th Chapter, Part II of the Constitution, treating of *Manual Labor, Spiritual Entertainments* and *Conferences*.

(12.) Let all repair to the Choir, precisely at three o'clock, to say Vespers and Complin; on Sundays and festivals, these are to be said a quarter before three. The time from

Vespers until four o'clock, both on Sundays and week-days, may be taken for a little relaxation.

(13.) From four o'clock until five, repair to the Community-room for manual labor; a half-hour is to be devoted to Spiritual Reading or some other pious exercise, at which all must assist as punctually as possible. On Sundays and festivals the Novices shall there recite Catechism, or do what their Mistress thinks proper. Each Choir-Sister should, in this assembly, say a word of edification, taken from the Catechism or any other pious book. When there is a sermon, this will supply for the spiritual conference. The Superioress may occasionally dispense with this assembly, which should never last more than half an hour. The rest of the time before five o'clock may be employed in taking a little relaxation, or in attending to necessities.

(14.) At five o'clock, repair to the Choir, to make together a half-hour's Meditation, after which say Matins and Lauds consecutively. During Lent, the Sisters should go there a quarter before five on week-days, and at half-past four on festivals, to say

Complin, after which make a half-hour's Meditation, and then say Matins and Lauds, as mentioned above.

(15.) A little after six o'clock they shall go to supper, and then take recreation until eight o'clock. A half hour of this time should be devoted to manual labor.

(16.) At eight o'clock, repair to the Chapel for Night Prayer. Let them make their general Examination of conscience, listen to the reading of the points of Meditation, and observe strict silence until the following day. After Night Prayer, all should retire to their cells and be in bed by nine o'clock.

Observances for the Exterior.

(1.) Besides the fasts commanded by the Church, the Sisters should observe those prescribed by the Constitutions—from which they may, however, be dispensed by the Rev. Mother.

(2.) They shall take the discipline on Fridays, and never perform any extraordinary penance without permission. Let them observe silence during the time, and in the place prescribed, and never receive or send letters, or anything else, without permission. They must repair punctually to the different exercises of the Community at the first sound of the bell; be exact in the discharge of their duties, and obey each one in her employment.

(3.) Let them have nothing odd in their dress, and keep nothing in their rooms that savors of propriety or singularity without permission.

(4.) They must always wear their veil in the Parlor, where they should be accompanied by a Sister.

(5.) Let them go to Confession and Communion twice a week—on Sundays and Thursdays—when there is not another fast, and not oftener without permission.

(6.) The Sisters should, annually, make a retreat of about ten days; and, each month, take a day of recollection, if their health permit. The Novices shall do the same if they are able.

(7.) They should perform all their actions as directed, and through obedience. All should, at least once a month, make a manifestation of their interior to the Rev. Mother; and the Novices, every week, to their Mistress—exposing their temptations and difficulties, as prescribed in Chapter VII, Part I, of the Constitutions.

(8.) Should any one have contested or used harsh words towards any Sister, let her effect a reconciliation, and ask pardon on her knees.

Observances for the Interior.

(1.) The Sisters should daily make some special acts of love towards God; for instance, in the morning, after Meditation, during the Holy Sacrifice of the Mass, and during the hour of Retreat before dinner.

(2.) They should be especially careful to make three acts in honor of Jesus, our divine Saviour. Let the first be an act of adoration, acknowledging Him as our God and sovereign Lord, accepting Him in that quality, and wishing to depend on Him for our being, our actions, our life, and our eternity.

(3.) The second should be an act of entire and humble oblation of ourselves, as belonging to Him, because He has created us by His Power, redeemed us by His Goodness, and called us to His holy service by His grace. Let us, therefore, give ourselves to Him voluntarily, renouncing every right and all dominion that we have over ourselves and that which concerns us.

(4.) The third act should be to direct our intentions to God, referring to His glory, our life, our thoughts, words and actions; purposing to love Him eternally with all the powers of our soul, and to accomplish all our actions, especially those of the present day, for His love and in honor of His sovereign Majesty. Let us make similar acts, to honor the Blessed Virgin in her dignity of Mother of God, and the sovereignty which is attached to it; accepting her as our Queen, on whom we wish to depend in all that concerns us. Let us offer ourselves to her as having full right over us, that she may dispose of us as she pleases. Moreover, let us give her all the authority over us, that she had over the Son of God, who deigned to subject Himself to her as her Son; and offer her our intention of referring to her glory, after that of her divine

Son, all our thoughts, words and actions.

(5.) The Sisters should never permit a day to pass, without making these acts of adoration, and oblation, directing their intentions actually and interiorly, and offering them to Jesus and His Immaculate Mother at a specified time; for these three acts, together with that of love, express our greatest obligations in regard to God, and the main object of our sojourn on earth.

(6.) The Sisters should not permit two hours of the day to pass without raising their heart to God, by some act of love or of adoration.

(7.) Besides the general oblation of their actions in the morning, let the Sisters accustom themselves never to do anything of importance without first offering it to our Lord and His Blessed Mother, in union with, and in honor of the actions they performed while on earth, begging grace to perform the duty in question, as something belonging to them.

(8.) The Sisters should recall to mind the modesty with which the Son of God performed His actions while on earth, and to honor His humiliations, let them perform their actions with humility, modesty and tranquility.

(9.) When called to the Parlor, they should offer their conversation in honor of that which our Blessed Lord deigned to hold with men while on earth, beseeching Him to preserve them from vanity and dissipation of mind.

(10.) On entering or leaving their cells, they should say a short prayer before their Oratory, to renew or preserve the spirit of recollection, amid their exterior employments.

(11.) Before the Spiritual Reading let them raise their heart to God, imploring His light and grace to derive the fruits of His love from this pious exercise.

(12.) The Sisters should carefully exercise themselves in humility, charity, and simplicity. Let them be condescending towards all, and perform all their actions with charitable intentions in regard to one another and to the Community at large. They should make known their necessities and temptations to the Directors of their conscience with great simplicity.

(13.) Let the Sisters keep their souls in an interior retreat in God amidst their exterior occupations, employing for this end, the means proposed in general and private conferences. They shall daily make two Examinations of Conscience; the first in the forenoon, after the Litany of the Blessed Virgin; at which they are to renew their fervor in the love and service of our Lord and His holy Mother; applying themselves to the acquisition of the virtue they have proposed to themselves for the week, in honor of some similar virtue or perfection practised by Jesus and Mary, while on earth. The second examination shall be made in the evening after the recreation; at this time, they should place themselves before our Lord as criminals, with such sentiments as if they were to die and be judged during that very hour.

(14.) Never pass a day without some particular homage to the mystery of the Incarnation, recalling the great part the Blessed Virgin acted in this mystery, and the homage which she paid it. For this intention, the Sisters may say three *Paters* and *Aves*, or any other prayer.

(15.) Besides the general offering which the Sisters should make of their sleep to Jesus and Mary, as the Sovereigns of every action of their life, it would be well, in order to compensate for the long time they pass in sleep, without raising their hearts to God, to beg the Saints, to whom they have a special devotion, to love God for them, in order that, not being able to make acts of love themselves, they may, at least, do so in the person of others.

(16.) Let the Sisters never pass a day without doing something to honor the Passion of our Lord; it would be well, therefore, to practise some interior or exterior acts of mortification. Perhaps it would be *a propos* to deprive themselves of something at each meal, either in quality or in quantity,—in order that, while necessity compels them to give nature what it requires, their love for the Son of God will induce them thus to prove their gratitude for innumerable benefits received.

A. M. D. G. ET S. C. J. G.

CONTENTS.

	PAGE.
Approbation of the Translation..	5
Approbation of the Original Constitutions............................	5
Approbation of the Revised Edition, 1827................................	7
Preface..	9
The Rule of Our Father St. Augustin..	13
Introduction to the Constitutions..	25

PART I.

CHAPTER.	PAGE.
I.—On the Charity towards God, Recommended in the Rule	28
II.—On Charity towards our Neighbor and Perfect Union Among the Sisters...	32
III.—Formulæ for the Religious Profession and the Renewal of Vows..	37
IV.—On Poverty...	43
V.—On Chastity..	48
VI.—On Obedience..	52
VII.—Retreat and Solitude..	58
VIII.—The Time of Silence and the Hour of Retreat............	62
IX.—Penances, Abstinence and Mortification........................	66
X.—Humility..	74
XI.—On Piety and the Exercises it Ordains..........................	79
XII.—Religious Modesty..	85
XIII.—Mental Prayer..	90
XIV.—Confession and Holy Communion................................	95
XV.—Dispositions requisite for a good Confession...............	100
XVI.—Dispositions for Holy Communion..............................	104
XVII.—The Divine Office..	109
XVIII.—The Prayers and Good Works to be Offered for the Souls of the Deceased Sisters, Founders and Benefactors of the House...	114

PART II.

CHAPTER.	PAGE.
I.—On Cloister, the Entrance and the Parlors...................	119
II.—The Refectory, the Repast and Recreation..................	126
III.—The Dormitory, the Cells and Repose...........................	132
IV.—The Infirmary and the Care of the Sick......................	136
V.—Of Manual Labor and Spiritual Conferences...............	141

CHAPTER.	PAGE.
VI.—The Chapter and Fraternal Correction	145
VII.—The Temporal Administration	156
VIII.—The Reception and Training of Novices	163
IX.—The Lay-Sisters	173
X.—The Lodging, Reception and Instruction of the Boarders	176
XI.—The Day-School and Sunday-School	179
XII.—The Pastoral Visitation	186

PART III.

CHAPTER.	PAGE.
I.—General Dispositions for the various Offices in the Monastery	189
II.—The Election of the Superioress and Assistant	193
III.—The Mother Superioress	204
IV.—The Assistant	219
V.—The Treasurer	225
VI.—The Counsellors	231
VII.—The Mistress of Novices	234
VIII.—The Sister Portress	247
IX.—The Housekeeper	251
X.—The Directress of the Academy	256
XI.—The Zelatrice	259
XII.—The Sacristan	262
XIII.—The Directress of the Choir	267
XIV.—The Infirmarian	271
XV.—The Minor Employments	278
XVI.—Dispositions for the Employments of the Lay-Sisters	287
XVII.—The Obligation of the Sisters to Observe the Constitutions	288
Remarks on the Instructions	293
Conclusion	294
Directory containing the Daily Exercises, Practices and Customs	296

Laus Deo!

www.ingramcontent.com/pod-product-compliance
Lightning Source LLC
Chambersburg PA
CBHW031907220426
43663CB00006B/798